A Search for Environmental Ethics
An Initial Bibliography

A Search for
ENVIRONMENTAL ETHICS
An Initial Bibliography

Compiled by

Mary Anglemyer

Eleanor R. Seagraves

Catherine C. LeMaistre

Under the auspices of

Rachel Carson Council, Inc.

With an Introduction by

S. Dillon Ripley

Smithsonian Institution Press

Washington, D.C., 1980

Library of Congress Cataloging in Publication Data
Anglemyer, Mary
A search for environmental ethics.
Includes indexes.
1. Nature conservation—Moral and religious aspects—
Bibliography. 2. Environmental protection—Moral
and religious aspects—Bibliography. 3. Ecology—
Moral and religious aspects—Bibliography. 4. Human
ecology—Moral and religious aspects—Bibliography.
5. Bioethics—Bibliography. I. Seagraves, Eleanor R.,
joint author. II. LeMaistre, Catherine C., joint author.
III. Title.
Z7405.N38A53   [QH75]   016.3042′8   80-15026
ISBN 0-87474-212-9

Rachel Carson Council, Inc.
8940 Jones Mill Road
Washington, D.C. 20015

Preparation of this bibliography was made possible
in part by a grant from the
United States Environmental Protection Agency.

Contents

Introduction

For a hundred years and more, there have been people in the sciences, and in philosophy and religion, who have considered problems in environmental ethics. It is, however, the period since World War II that has produced persistent evidence of environmental imbalance on a global scale. A much wider audience is now aware that the future of the human race may depend on the degree to which we comprehend the intricacies of the ecological network.

The year 1950 marked the beginning of my own interest in conservation. As an ornithologist working in biology, I had thought of conservationists as people who kept bird lists but did not care about bird scientists, who went to bird-club meetings once a year, and railed at politicians and land despoilers.

I began to realize that at the rate at which human population was increasing and exploiting the land, natural habitats would be so severely depleted by the turn of the century that much of the end products of evolution—the thousands of species of birds, the millions of species of other animals, each closely adapted to its own ecosystem—would cease to exist.

My first concern was for the genetic waste, the fact that these end products of adaptation would be snuffed out before we, as human observers, would know what it was that in fact they represented. Conservation thus meant to me the preservation of a mosaic of habitats in which could be preserved at least a broad cross section of species which would act as reservoirs for accumulating a further storehouse of information. I felt that it was imperative that biologists who knew the facts should somehow make themselves known to conservationists, if only to advise them and keep them on the right track.

Meanwhile, the tangled skeins of pollution evolving from urban sprawl, industrialization, and overpopulation began to be more and more apparent across the face of the world. From the sheltered confines of the laboratory or the museum, biologists could look out on a situation for which they were hardly prepared. Ecology had suddenly become an urgent area, as urgent as biomedical research.

Now, if ever, we must begin to realize what the ecologists and the evolutionists have long sensed: the biosphere is all one; the realms of species are finite; the ecosystems interdigitate. The quality of life turns out to be not simply a romantic ideal, but a set of standards, still intangible, still highly arguable, on which to base survival. Man as a population is very directly an environmental component, just like domestic animals, wild-animal species, and plants.

7

To maintain a large, growing, human population in harmony with the environment requires an historical perspective of human societies in their natural surroundings. Today we are witnesses to the aftereffects of our own ability to change the environment in a monumental sense. For the first time people have the technological means to create mega-changes in the environment.

I would say that on the one hand careless technology in the more developed countries that may be viewed as reckless by the less developed countries is matched by the careless population increase of the less developed countries. The human race has no divine right to overlook ecological principles. If it does, all the technological dreams of the future, the succession of new solutions round the corner, can only turn to ashes in the mouth.

Where then to turn? How can we possibly develop answers, for the long haul, to reactions in nature which will satisfy American impatience? It is part and parcel of our instinct in regard to government policy to put out brush fires that developed last year rather than attempt to plan for the next ones that may break out three or four years from now.

In such an atmosphere, government activity occurs by inertia. Only a shock of some sort will produce a response, often a twitch as if the body were asleep. Collectively perhaps this is a wise maneuver, for overreaction sometimes exacerbates the cause of the trouble in the first place. Meanwhile, however, conservation of itself is overlooked. The influences which affect conservation adversely continue to grow and develop. Human population pressure increases relentlessly, and at the same time human expectations continue to rise as education and the spread of communications develop.

Today conservation directly affects the well-being of the human community. Destroying the variety of species (and their habitats) is economically prodigal. It closes off mankind's options and it removes tools a scientist may well need to serve humanity. We now realize that it will require careful planning to maintain the necessary diversity in living environments.

If endangered species and their habitats, like the air we breathe and the water we drink, can be thought of as common resources of mankind, then they too can serve to illuminate other dimensions of the complexities of common property resources. They often represent the conflict between personal advantage and community loss—the difference, for example, between exploitation and conservation of international ecosystems like the oceans.

In all of this there is an enormous gap between the "have" and the "have-not" nations. Most of the ardent conservationists are in the "have" nations and are therefore suspect to the rest of the world. Is this concern with the environment a kind of neoimperialism? Do the "haves" really care? It is far more complex to reason that the rare species and habitats of the world are international common property, like the seabed, part of the patrimony of mankind owned by the community of the world. Like owners of a growth stock, we should be wise to the future, aware of the past, and should distrust those who would say "grab ye a profit while ye may."

The planet may spin but we are not aware of it. In the slow turning of the earth, the ineffably minute changes that collectively make a difference become meaningless to us. So what if we read that fifty acres of tropical forest are being destroyed each minute, or each hour, or each day. What does that have to do with us? Someone else will notice it eventually. It seems as inconceivable that such a statistic could ever affect us as that some day we would be issued the last gallon of gas that we would use—ever.

I believe there is one ethic, one principle left out of our consciousness. It is conservation. It is perhaps the last larger responsibility, bigger than us all. Museum people are singularly reminded of mortality, like priests and doctors, by the deterioration of objects created by the hand of man. Is it possible to transfer this reminder to the rest of our known space, the earth itself? Conservation of that which we ourselves had no part in creating is an even greater moral charge. It is a harder task, for it is all the more impersonal. We can care for our own possessions, our house, our cave, and we can fight for our allotment, our quarter acre, but can we bring ourselves to feel responsible for all of nature in the context of time? It is an impersonal, larger responsibility, but it is incumbent on us all, now that we know for the first time we have tipped the scales, changing it all inexorably in a time frame which is not apparent to our generation.

Today there is no nation in the world which has not been affected in varying degree by scientific and technological interests and by communications systems that speed the dissemination of information to and from the farthest corners of the earth. Formulating principles of conservation in a complicated world requires that we retrieve and share something of the deep sense of mystery found in the unity of all life on this planet; and this sense underlies both science and religious faith.

This bibliography addresses this responsibility and aims to aid in the search for an environmental ethic. Small and highly selective though it is, it provides for the first time a reference guide to the diverse literature on this important topic.

S. Dillon Ripley, Secretary
Smithsonian Institution

Preface

This bibliography is intended as a guide for persons looking for references on environmental ethics. The materials encompassed here are extensive. However, a few considerations—availability of titles and time allotted—limited the effort.

Scope: The natural environment is the focal point of this bibliography. Selections reflect the attitudes of diverse groups and individuals toward that environment and the roles of humans as both protectors and users of the earth's resources. Works in science, philosophy, religion, education, literature, politics, and economics (wherever it touches on conservation-environmental values) are described. Social issues, though not ignored, are included only where the main emphasis is on the natural environment. Only publications in the English language are included.

Coverage begins with the end of World War II. Since then modern economic and social patterns have become firmly established. Science and technology complemented public demands for consumer goods, which had been scarce since the Great Depression of the 1930s. The baby boom of the 1950s accelerated the need for food, water, housing, and energy supplies. A few foresighted people recognized the limitations of the earth's resources and the risks inherent in a consumer-dominated life style. They began pressing for public understanding of the need to conserve so that future generations would have the opportunity, not only to survive, but to enjoy a life in balance with ecological realities. Their emphasis on moral and ethical principles provided a stimulus for environmental appreciation.

Arrangement and Style: Items in this bibliography appear alphabetically either by author (individual or corporate), editor, or title. Entries for monographs provide author and/or editor, title, place, publisher, date, number of pages. Those for journal articles supply author and title, title of the journal, volume, issue, date, and inclusive paging. Where copies of a work can be obtained only from a particular source, that name and address is given.

Indexes: The Subject Index is arranged alphabetically. Obvious general words—ecology, environment, ethics, morals, nature—are omitted: all the entries are concerned with some or all of these topics. Philosophy and Theology are listed for titles that refer specifically to these disciplines. Religion and Christianity are omitted because references to them are numerous; other specific religions are identified, e.g., Buddhism. The word "church" is used in its institutional sense.

The Name Index lists individual and corporate names not appearing as primary authors. Thus, for all coverage of cited references to a particular person or organization, it is necessary to check the Name Index as well as the bibliography itself.

Sources Consulted: An alphabetical list of institutions appears at the end of the bibliography.

Acknowledgments: Many individuals from various professional fields generously responded to our inquiries with helpful suggestions. We are grateful to all who took the time to give us titles of works they found influential for their own thinking.

A note of appreciation must be made to: the Library of Congress, where much of the delving was done; the National Wildlife Federation, which contributed both ideas and practical assistance; the Denver Public Library's Conservation Library, which provided us with print-outs from their data bases; the Smithsonian Institution, whose Secretary, S. Dillon Ripley, graciously contributed the introduction; the staff of the Smithsonian Institution Press, whose interest substantially increased the usefulness of this volume; and the officers and staff of the Rachel Carson Council, under whose auspices this work originated. Special credit goes to the U. S. Environmental Protection Agency, and particularly to Joan Martin Nicholson, Director of the Office of Public Awareness, whose support and encouragement gave the impetus for this project.

Users may find some of their favorite titles missing; we hope that in these cases, they will assist us by submitting such titles to the Council in the event that another edition of this bibliography is planned.

Bibliography

• 1. Abrecht, Paul. **Technology: New Directions in Ecumenical Social Ethics.** Christianity and Crisis 35(7) April 28, 1975: 92–98.
Article expounding reasons for the church to enter into a dialogue with technologists and scientists to challenge some long-standing ideologies and social patterns supporting the "irreversible" character and development of technology. How long can we continue to think of man, nature, and God as individual categories with separate purviews? The connection between technology and society is also discussed in relation to developing countries in Africa and Asia.

2. Alexander, Hartley B. **The World's Rim: Great Mysteries of the North American Indians.** Lincoln: University of Nebraska Press, 1953. 259 p.
Studies of Native American rituals and ceremonies; with interpretations by the author, who also traces analogies (but not origins) to classical Old World cosmogonies. Many of these ceremonies are connected with Indian beliefs in the oneness of life.

• 3. Allen, Diogenes. **Theological Reflection on the Natural World.** Theology Today 25(4) January 1969: 435–445.
A philosopher takes theologians to task for concentrating only on human relations with God. He believes there is good reason to affirm that the entire universe is dependent on God and that that principle should be studied in any attempt to understand history, society, and human nature. Index.

4. Allen, Durward L. **Our Wildlife Legacy.** Rev. ed. New York: Funk and Wagnalls, 1962. 422 p.
The author's object is to provide the public with a guide to wildlife conservation (interpreted as wise use), philosophy, and practice. A history of American management and mismanagement of its wildlife, with specific examples, forms the main body of the work. The final chapters suggest principles on which improved management practices can be based and how these can promote a better standard of living and quality of life. Extensive notes; bibliography; index.

5. Allsopp, Bruce. **The Garden Earth: The Case for Ecological Morality.** New York: Morrow, 1972. 117 p.
This is the age of the "rapacious society." Ironically, we educate youth

13

for self-development in a "world in which self-fulfillment becomes increasingly difficult." With modern conditions in mind, Allsopp analyzes the functional nature of morality, the meaning of ecological ethics, and the wide spectrum of social and individual responsibility to the environment. Notes and index.

● 6. Alpers, Kenneth P. **Toward an Environmental Ethic.**
Dialog 15(1) Winter 1976: 49–55.
An article examining historical and theological interpretations of North American "belief-systems and ethics" as they relate to the land on which we have spread our civilization and from which we draw nourishment. The "Ethic of Conquest" is followed by a look at two American thought patterns: "Nature as Sacred," and "Nature as Neutral to Man." Finally, Alpers elaborates on the "Ecological Perspective" and "An Ethic for the Care of the Earth," noting that two Christian concepts must be rethought—asceticism and stewardship. Notes.

7. **Alternatives to Growth-1: A Search for Sustainable Futures.** Edited by Dennis L. Meadows. Papers adapted from entries to the 1975 George and Cynthia Mitchell Prize and from presentations before the 1975 Alternatives to Growth Conference held at The Woodlands, Texas. Cambridge, Mass.: Ballinger, 1977. 405 p.
Essays by a group of businessmen, educators, and futurists on designing a steady-state society. In his introduction, the editor summarizes ten themes common to these papers. The first is the need to preserve and to have contacts with the natural ecosystem. Part IV, "Life-styles and Social Norms for a Sustainable State," examines current patterns, laws, and religions and suggests new ways of thinking and innovative educational programs and life styles. Bibliography; biographical notes on contributors; and complete list of conference papers.

8. **America's Changing Environment.** Daedalus 96(4) Fall 1967: iii–viii, 1003–1225.
Fifteen articles that discuss cross currents of political and economic thought and planning for the decade, 1967–77, as they relate to resources, conservation, recreation, and environmental education.

9. **America's Changing Environment.** Edited by Roger Revelle and Hans H. Landsberg. Boston: Houghton, 1970. 314 p.
A collection of essays on many aspects of life in the United States and on factors contributing to decision making in environmental matters. In their introduction, the editors debate the issues and question traditional methods of reaching decisions. Several authors propose changes in our

values and priorities. Others deal with the technical, social, political, and economic ramifications of reversing trends responsible for the environment's steady deterioration. References at the end of each chapter; index.

10. Ashby, Eric. **Towards an Environmental Ethic.** Nature 262(5564) July 8, 1976: 84–85.
Using recent works in science and law on the principles of decision making in environmental matters as guides, Ashby traces the evolution of an environmental ethic.

11. Atkinson, J. Brooks. **This Bright Land: A Personal View.** Drawings by Earl Thollander. Published for the American Museum of Natural History. Garden City, N.Y.: Doubleday, 1972. 201 p.
Essays by a *New York Times* writer on the natural history, current conditions, and moral lessons of this country. He assumes that the Bible promised humans domination and that we still believe nature is for our exclusive use and control. As long as we continue in this vein, we are destroying our own environment.

12. **The Atmosphere: Endangered and Endangering.** Edited by William W. Kellogg and Margaret Mead. [Bethesda, Md.] The National Institutes of Health, 1977. 154 p.
Papers from a 1977 conference at the National Institute of Environmental Health Services, Research Triangle Park, N.C., sponsored by that Institute and the Fogarty International Center. In the Preface Margaret Mead points out that the decisions which society must make can endanger the whole planet. Therefore, it is imperative that scientists, technologists, and political leaders maintain close communication, keeping in mind their ethical responsibilities. Some of the especially pertinent papers are in part 3: "Human Costs and Benefits of Environmental Change . . ." and in part 5: "Will Mankind Behave Rationally?" Bibliography; glossary; index.
Available from Superintendent of Documents, U. S. Government Printing Office, catalog no. HE20.3710.39.

13. Baer, Richard A. **Higher Education: The Church and Environmental Values.** Natural Resources Journal 17(3) July 1977: 477–491.
An educator discusses the two institutions from which changes in perception of, and reaction to, environment must come. The teaching of utilitarian philosophies must be balanced by opportunities to learn other values. The church might reexamine its biblical heritage to bolster a moral impetus for preserving nature.

14. ———. **Our Need to Control: Implications for Environmental Education.** American Biology Teacher 38(8) November 1976: 473–476, 490.

In this article, Baer examines what he calls "the compulsive need in western culture to exercise control over the world." To counter this compulsion, which dominates our actions and is responsible for environmental degradation and human suffering, he proposes a broader concept of education. It would include contemplation and how to listen, be more sensitive, reflect on the mysteries of life—and especially—how to enjoy knowledge, not use it for manipulation.

15. Barbour, Ian G. **Issues in Science and Religion.** Englewood Cliffs, N.J.: Prentice-Hall, 1966. 470 p.

Barbour formulates essential questions on the subject. The study has several divisions and examines in detail these three topics: "methods of inquiry in science and religion; man's relation to nature; and God's relation to nature." See especially the final section and conclusions, "Toward a Theology of Nature."

16. ———, ed. **Western Man and Environmental Ethics: Attitudes Toward Nature and Theology.** Reading, Mass.: Addison-Wesley, 1973. 276 p.

This collection of essays reflects a range of opinions on the theory of stewardship vs. domination in Judeo-Christian thinking. In his summary, Barbour concludes that while differences exist, the consensus is recognition of the interdependence of all forms of life, and that the various disciplines of the human mind can contribute to their preservation.

17. Barker, Edwin, ed. **The Responsible Church.** London: S.P.C.K., Holy Trinity Church, 1966. 90 p.

Essays. See especially the last, "Man's Dominion," by Hugh Montefiore. Given human dominion over nature, what then have we done to develop a sense of responsibility for the care of God's gifts? If little so far, what are the long-term consequences in a world where consumption of natural resources is growing and where many contaminants are inadequately controlled?

18. Barker, Elmer E. [**Editorial**] The Living Wilderness 12(22) Autumn 1947: [1].

Short credo for conservationists who teach equal respect for, and responsibility toward, all of earth's creatures and creations.

19. Barnes, Irston R. **The Quest for a Conservation Ethic.** Atlantic Naturalist 14(3) July–September 1959: 194–198.

Existing confusion over conservation policy is seen largely as a result of the intrusion of economics and politics into what is fundamentally a question of ethics. Barnes finds exact parallels between the Christian and the conservation ethic; he illustrates the latter with quotations from Aldo Leopold.

20. Barnette, Henlee H. **The Church and the Ecological Crisis.** Grand Rapids, Mich.: Eerdmans, 1972. 114 p.
A concise volume designed to help the churchman assess salient factors of the ecological crisis and related theological and ethical perspectives. Causative elements of the crisis (population growth, among others) as well as survival strategies are outlined. Many disciplines and pressure groups engage in the debate. The appendixes include a discussion of evil and nature; a sermon by John R. Claypool, "The Theology of Ecology"; and a list of books and films.

21. Barney, Daniel R. **The Last Stand: Ralph Nader's Group Report on the National Forests.** New York: Grossman, 1974. 185 p.
In his introduction, Nader points to the conflict of values surrounding America's forest resources and the difficulties the U. S. Forest Service has in keeping to its original ideology—the preservation of the nation's forests. The book reports the historical debate over the Forest Service's mandate and its conflicting legacies. Also discussed are the clearcutting of timber; threats to recreational areas, wildlife habitats and ranges; and recent recognition of public demands for a "land ethic" approach to Forest Service management. Appendixes; notes; index.

22. Bates, Marston. **The Forest and the Sea: A Look at the Economy of Nature and the Ecology of Man.** New York: Random House, 1960. 278 p.
Bates defines biology as the science of all living things, separated into special disciplines for human convenience but, in reality, a unified whole. The final chapter, "Man's Place in Nature," emphasizes that human destiny is tied to that of nature and that we must be wary of allowing ourselves to be distanced from the natural environment by the allure of social, technological, and historical power. Notes and index.

23. ——. **Man in Nature.** 2d ed. Englewood Cliffs, N.J.: Prentice-Hall, 1961. 116 p. (Foundations of Modern Biology Series)
Part of a series designed to assist biology teachers in presenting their classes with basic, modern, and dynamic aspects of the science. His approach allows for discussions of population dynamics, agricultural biology, ecology of disease, the economy of nature, resources, and wildlife management, among other topics. He concludes with a philosophical section on values of biology and of knowledge about the human role in nature. Photographs and illustrations; index.

17

24. Bateson, Gregory. **Mind and Nature: A Necessary Unity.**
New York: Dutton, 1979. 230 p.

A work encompassing a lifetime of study and teaching in biology, cybernetics, anthropology, psychiatry, and other social sciences while searching for the "patterns which connect" all living things in biological evolution. Bateson is concerned that while occidental educators teach the latest factual knowledge, it is rare that any one examines the universal connections between mind and matter or explores the "mental process" in nature. The false perception we have of our ability to transform the natural world threatens the "survival of the whole biosphere." The appendix is a reprint of his essay, "Time Is out of Joint," delivered to the University of California Committee on Educational Policy, July 20, 1978. Glossary and index.

25. Batisse, Michel. **Environmental Problems and the Scientist.** Bulletin of the Atomic Scientists 29(2) February 1973: 15–21.

Based on a lecture by the Director of Natural Resources Research, UNESCO, at the 12th Pacific Science Congress held at Australian National University, Canberra. The article suggests that scientists can contribute substantially to the development of new social ethics to provide a reasonably good quality of life. Batisse feels that principles are needed for a "new deal" between humans and nature, one in which partnership supplants domination while aiming at equity, justice, and unity among the world's peoples.

26. Bernos de Gasztold, Carmen. **Prayers from the Ark.**
Translated [from the French] by Rumer Godden.
Illustrations by Jean Primrose. New York: Viking, 1962.
71 p.

This poet believes that birds, animals, and insects are very much a part of God's world, as He saved them in the ark; hence they feel free to petition His grace on their lives.

27. ———. **The Creatures' Choir.** Translated [from the French] by Rumer Godden. Illustrations by Jean Primrose. New York: Viking, 1965. 69 p.

A companion to *Prayers from the Ark.*

● 28. Berry, Wendell. **A Continuous Harmony: Essays Cultural and Agricultural.** New York: Harcourt, 1972. 182 p.

Essays that touch several aspects of Westerners and how they look at the world: poets on nature themes; what happens to vision in "societies of waste"; some disciplines and some hopes. See especially the essay, "Think Little," a basis in ethics, pp. 71–85.

29. ———. **The Unsettling of America: Culture and Agriculture.** San Francisco: Sierra Club, 1977. 228 p.

A poet, teacher, and farmer, Berry traces the historical roots of industrial economics—a force that has long dominated American culture and affected its land. A "mentality of exploitation" continues to grow with the development of modern corporate agri-businesses and the influences of the petro-chemical industry on farming. The decrease in "nurtured" farms (except among small, cohesive groups like the Amish) is a change in which humans are cut off from the land or from caring how anyone uses it. At the same time, the general population is encouraged to eat adulterated, "efficiency" foods and to waste resources that are finite. Notes.

30. Beston, Henry. **The Outermost House: A Year of Life on the Great Beach of Cape Cod.** New ed. New York: Holt, 1949. 222 p.

A year spent alone on the sea's edge gives this naturalist time to reflect on, and record his belief in, "the divine mystery" of nature and of humanity.

31. Bethge, Eberhard. **Ethics.** *In* his Dietrich Bonhoeffer . . . Translated [from the German] by Eric Mosbacher and others. Edited by Edwin Robertson. London: Collins, 1970. pp. 619–626.

A brief comment by Bethge on the work Bonhoeffer intended to be the culmination of his theology but which he was unable to finish before his execution by the Nazis. We glimpse Bonhoeffer's interpretation of the world and the place of human beings within it as a mandate from God through Christ.

32. **Bill Turnage Talks About Wilderness, A Land Ethic and Challenges Ahead.** Interview by Robert Cahn. The Living Wilderness 43(145) June 1979: 15–19.

The Executive Director of The Wilderness Society discusses the philosophical base of the conservation movement in the United States and finds hope that present and future Americans will adapt an ethical viewpoint toward the environment. He also presents plans for the Society to stimulate that concern.

33. Black, John. **The Dominion of Man: The Search for Ecological Responsibility.** Edinburgh: The University Press, 1970. 169 p.

Revised and expanded from a course of three lectures in conservation titled "Western Worldview and the Inevitability of the Ecological Crisis." It presents an overview consisting of philosophical and biblical background, and political and scientific influences. This is a study of the complex set of "ideas on which western civilization is based" and the effects upon stewardship concepts, private property rights, and the future of Western civilization. Bibliography and index.

34. Blackburn, Joyce. **The Earth is the Lord's?** Waco, Tex.: Word Books, 1972. 160 p.

From her experience in battling to save the Marshes of Glynn, Blackburn is convinced that the answer to the title's question is emphatically yes. She urges us to use the gifts of grace and love in ameliorating the effects of environmental crises so we may continue to enjoy God's creation. She suggests sources for self-education, poems for contemplation, and activities in which to participate.

35. Blackstone, William T., ed. **Philosophy and Environmental Crisis.** Athens: University of Georgia Press, 1974. 140 p.

Eight papers delivered at the Fourth Annual Conference in Philosophy, University of Georgia, February 18–20, 1971. Zoologist-ecologist Eugene Odum describes the need to continue the evolution of human ethics. He suggests we extend religious value systems based on man-to-man and man-to-society obligations to include the ethical relationship of humans to their environment. The seven essays by American philosophers that follow explore and weigh the values and social and economic habits that bear upon human interests and preferences. Questions posed include: Must ethical evaluations be man-centered? Do animals and unborn generations have rights? What are the legal and moral aspects of world population pressures?

36. **Blueprint for Survival.** By the editors of The Ecologist, Edward Goldsmith, and others. Boston: Houghton, 1972. 189 p.

The staff of "The Ecologist" expanded into this book their theories for global ecological planning. The magazine version caused great comment at the United Nations Conference on the Human Environment in Stockholm, 1972.

37. Bok, Sissela and Callahan, Daniel. **Teaching Applied Ethics.** Radcliffe Quarterly 65(2) June 1979: 30–33.

In addition to the perennial, individual moral choices, society now faces social choices on a massive scale. Among these are energy ethics and the husbanding of global resources. This fact has spurred a revival of graduate and undergraduate courses in ethics. The authors stress that these must be carefully developed and responsibly administered to provide the tools for moral choices and decisions.

38. Bonifazi, Conrad. **A Theology of Things: A Study of Man in his Physical Environment.** Philadelphia: Lippincott, 1967. 237 p.

A scholarly exploration of religious and philosophical concepts by a Christian theologian. Bonifazi discusses many responses between human groups and the natural world from biblical times to Teilhard de Chardin. These emanate from philosophy, religion, science, literature, and the mysterious language of the spirit—all of which manifest human awareness of the existing world. Footnotes and index.

39. Bourjaily, Vance. **The Unnatural Enemy.** New York: Dial Press, 1963. 182 p.

A novelist and hunter examines the myths and realities of hunting in the American Midwest. He shows the wide range of prevailing attitudes and conditions, from careful, sportsmanlike forays in the fields near his home to the mass slaughter of goose-shooting at Cairo, Illinois. Examples more than precepts define Bourjaily's ethic of man and his quarry.

40. Bowden, Gerald. **Protecting Our Environment Through Legislation: Approaching a New Concept of Property.** Real Estate Law Journal 4(2) Fall 1975: 165–180.

To achieve environmental quality, laws must be based on a consensus which requires a new philosophy of social obligations. A new concept of property rights must replace the present dictum of the private owner's right to absolute use and disposal of land.

41. Bowen, Murray. **Cultural Myths and the Realities of Problem-Solving.** Ekistics 37(220) March 1974: 173–179.

A psychiatrist presents a chilling forecast of forthcoming environmental disaster. He recommends priority research on the complex array of interactions between humans and their environment; better efforts by public educators to teach values concerning environmental harmony; and an ethical regard toward nature.

42. Boyd, Doug. **Rolling Thunder.** New York: Random House, 1974. 273 p.

A penetrating examination of the life and experiences of an American Indian medicine man, with frequent references to humans' respect for all creatures, nature, and the power of the Great Spirit over all.

43. Brennan, Matthew. **Editorial.** Journal of Environmental Education 7(4) Summer 1976: 65.

The executive editor urges restoration of conservation and nature study into the curriculum to give children an opportunity to explore—and become an integral part of—their environment.

44. Brewer, George E. **Towards a Conservation Ethic.**
Teachers College Record 64(4) January 1963: 279–289.
Through a history of the human race, Brewer shows how its development
has degraded the environment, and indeed humanity itself, particularly
in North America. He suggests several remedies, including Aldo Leopold's
"land ethic"; recognition of the unity of all life; and extending the concept
of ethics from humans to the entire biotic community.

45. Brockway, Allan R. **Toward a Theology of the Natural
World.** Engage/Social Action 1(7) July 1973: 21–30.
Brockway cites both early scripture and modern discussions of man vs.
nature themes. Some Native American religions illustrate a true recognition of, and reverence for, other forms of life, animate and inanimate.
Modern peoples of Judeo-Christian traditions may forget, but now must
reconsider, and perhaps reincorporate such a respect into their religion.

46. Brokaw, Howard P., ed. **Wildlife and America:
Contributions to an Understanding of American Wildlife and
its Conservation.** Washington, D.C.: U. S. Government
Printing Office, 1978. 532 p.
A study co-sponsored by the U. S. Council on Environmental Quality;
Fish and Wildlife Service; Forest Service; and National Oceanic and
Atmospheric Administration. It is a source book for facts and philosophy
about all of the nation's wild animals, be they vertebrate or invertebrate,
aquatic or terrestrial. It provides a critical analysis of the adequacy of
current conservation efforts. It is aimed at concerned individuals who
may read for information or pleasure; decision makers at all levels of
government who need an agenda for future actions; and professionals in
the natural resource management fields. Bibliographies and index.

47. Bronowski, Jacob. **A Sense of the Future: Essays in
Natural Philosophy.** Selected and edited by Piero E. Ariotti
in collaboration with Rita Bronowski. Cambridge, Mass.:
M.I.T. Press, 1977. 286 p.
This collection (from Bronowski's many publications from the early 1950s
until 1974) deals with the human values held by the scientists, humanists,
poets, and others who particularly contributed to his effort to "create a
philosophy for the 20th century which shall be all of one piece." The
articles, written from various angles of observation, comprise a cultural
and historical view of science and an assertion of its principles and hopes.

48. Brooks, David and Norman, Alma. **A Question of Choice.**
Alternatives 3(2) Winter 1974: 4–12.
The authors examine the kinds of choices forced upon us by the envi-
ronmental dilemma, focusing on the human rather than the environmental

impact. They conclude that, for humanitarian reasons, the way out of the dilemma is for each of us to stress conservation over consumption in our everyday decision making. They suggest we need to begin to "Listen to the poet as carefully as we do the engineer." Footnotes.

49. Brooks, Paul. **Roadless Area.** New York: Knopf, 1964. 260 p.

An account of personal visits to a number of diverse national parks, from St. John in the Virgin Islands to the open tundra of Mt. McKinley Park in Alaska. Wherever possible Brooks and his wife use natural means of transportation—canoeing, walking—to observe and to feel the effects of wilderness. The final chapter touches the theme of human kinship with nature and the contributions of science and the humanities to our understanding of this relationship. Appendixes.

50. Brower, David R., ed. **Not Man Apart: Lines From Robinson Jeffers.** Foreword by Loren Eiseley. New York: Ballantine, 1965. 160 p.

A Sierra Club Book combining Jeffers' poems with photographs of the Big Sur coast. These lines from the poem on the verso of the title page embody his passionate belief:

Integrity is wholeness,
the greatest beauty is
Organic wholeness, the wholeness of life and things,
the divine beauty of the universe.

51. ———, ed. **Wildlands in Our Civilization.** San Francisco: Sierra Club, 1964. 175 p.

Selected papers and discussions from the first five Biennial Wilderness Conferences, 1949–57. Compiled in memory of Howard Zahniser and in celebration of the passage of the Wilderness Act of 1964. Most of the papers consider the spiritual value of wilderness.

52. Brown, Lester R. **The Twenty-ninth Day: Accommodating Human Needs and Numbers to the Earth's Resources.** New York: Norton, 1978. 363 p.

A Worldwatch Institute Book. The first nine chapters cover the evidence of the rapid depletion of our natural resources and the human practices and conditions that cause this situation. The final three chapters are devoted to the need for accommodating with nature, a need which necessitates social and ethical change.

53. Browne, Stanley G. **Human Ecology, A Christian Concern.** London: Christian Medical Fellowship Publications, 1972. 22 p.

A British physician speaking to the Fellowship maintains that Christian doctors should become acquainted with the general lines of thinking on human ecology. Modern doctors must broaden their range of scientific and medical concern since they are inextricably bound up with all life in all parts of the world.

54. Brubaker, Sterling. **To Live on Earth: Man and His Environment in Perspective.** Baltimore: The Johns Hopkins Press, 1972. 202 p. (A Resources for the Future Study)

After observing that controlling the growth of population is the key to human survival on the planet, this study examines in some detail other significant areas of environmental threat and hazard. Included are many of the common impacts on the environment and strategies for coping. It focuses on the United States but does not neglect worldwide problems. Bibliography and index.

55. Brush, Edward H. **Iroquois: Past and Present.** New York: AMS Press, 1975. 96 p.

This reprint (from a text first published in Buffalo in 1901) recounts the visits of a white man to the Seneca country of western New York. It gives first-hand glimpses into religious or semi-religious ceremonies and functions that show the importance of nature, seasons, etc., in Indian rites. Of special interest to teachers is the free translation of the poem-prayer of Thanksgiving, pp. 71–73.

56. Buber, Martin. **I and Thou.** A new translation with a prologue, "I and You," and notes by Walter Kaufman. New York: Scribner, 1970. 185 p.

A profound philosophical treatise on the essence and nature of 'being' in the actual world. The work evokes experiences in the possibilties among humans of understanding essential realities. See especially, "I Contemplate a Tree" in the first part of the essay.

57. Burghardt, W. J. **Towards Reconciliation.** Washington, D.C.: United States Catholic Conference, 1974. 37 p.

Each chapter in this booklet touches on the origin of rupture and the need for reconciliation between God and humans, among people, and between people and nature. In the latter, the doctrine of stewardship is expounded. The final chapter indicates some appropriate actions. References.

Available from the publisher, 1312 Massachusetts Ave., N.W., Washington, D.C. 20005.

58. Byron, William J. **Toward Stewardship: An Interim Ethic of Poverty, Pollution and Power.** New York: Paulist Press, 1975. 89 p.

A simple, moral guide, drawn from biblical passages, showing the way to care for the earth and for the poor and thus attain the freedom to which humanity is entitled. The author uses the word "interim" to indicate that a new ethic is needed immediately and cannot wait for universal understanding and acceptance.

59. CCTA/IUCN Symposium on the Conservation of Nature and Natural Resources in Modern African States, Arusha, Tanganyika, 1961. **Report.** . . Morges, Switzerland: International Union for the Conservation of Nature and Natural Resources, 1963. 367 p.

The Food and Agriculture Organization of the United Nations (FAO) and the United Nations Educational, Scientific and Cultural Organization (UNESCO) organized the Symposium; publication of the ensuing report was made possible by UNESCO. The report consists of short presentations of the main topics, followed by the complete papers arranged alphabetically by author. The theme is the necessity to preserve Africa's flora, fauna, and habitats both as a continuing economic and cultural resource and to avoid a biological catastrophe. International and African speakers frequently refer to wildlife as sources of inspiration and well-being and pledge themselves to preservation for the benefit of future generations. Photographs.

60. Cahn, Robert. **Footprints on the Planet: A Search for an Environmental Ethic.** Foreword by Jacques Cousteau. New York: Universe, 1978. 277 p.

A sometimes exciting, sometimes depressing account of attitudes of government, business, organizations, and individuals toward the environment. Cahn, an investigative reporter, finds that some corporations, in response to pressure, have included environmental concerns in their internal discussions, but these rarely influence company policy. Several chapters provide a capsule history on the role of government at various levels and on the role of pressure groups in decision making. He comments that the churches have not followed the religious leaders who are strong advocates of an environmental ethic. There are case studies on AMAX, Weyerhauser, General Motors, and Cummins Engine Co., among the industries; on the Nature Conservancy and the Trust for Public Land as effective organizations; on the Green Gulch Ranch and Briarpatch Network as examples of alternative technologies and simple living. Finally there are brief notes on famous writers, from George P. Marsh to Rachel Carson and later.

25

61. ———. **The God Committee.** Audubon 81(3)
    May 1979: 10, 13.
A review of the Endangered Species Act of 1973 after it had been amended; of two actions brought under it; and reactions to the decisions. Cahn is fearful for the future of the Act, as environmental ethics are not as pervasive as they should be.

62. Calder, Nigel. **The Environment Game.** London: Panther
    Books, 1967. 191 p.
A science writer proposes a curious, utopian solution to the world's inability to feed large numbers of people adequately: develop the technology to produce food by factory methods. In any case, Calder says, "Even the simplest agriculture is a violation of nature." The idea is to eliminate the risk of hunger by relying on synthetic foods, thus allowing agricultural lands to return to a natural state or to be used by people for recreational purposes.

63. Caras, Roger. **Death as a Way of Life.** Boston: Little
    Brown, 1970. 173 p.
Hunting—at first necessary for food and clothing and now a far different matter as we stalk game with powerful rifles more for sport than need— is considered from many standpoints to discover what place it presently has in the human mind and senses. The author concludes with an analysis of why people hunt.

64. Carlson, Mark. **Churches and the Public Interest**
    Movement: . . . Helena, Mont.: Northern Rockies Action
    Group, Inc., 1979. 31 p.
Though addressing in particular the institutional Christian church in his region (the Northern Rockies), this environmentalist suggests that persons of all faiths should encourage their respective religious organizations to combine moral attention and institutional action to steer society toward ecological sanity. Carlson sees too much "privatization of religion," and not enough realization that a climate of greater trust and cooperation between religious and social interest groups can help us overcome divisiveness, especially now that environmental crisis is upon us. Some approaches toward this end are suggested.
    Available from the publisher at 9 Placer St., Helena, Mont. 59601.

65. Carr, Archie. **Ulendo: Travels of a Naturalist in and out**
    of Africa. New York: Knopf, 1964. 272 p.
Ulendo is a Chunyanja word for journey. Carr takes the reader not only into remote parts of Africa, but back through distant ages to discover the essence of many forms of life and their evolutionary significance. As we watch, the spectacle is being destroyed: ". . . and the last great fantasy

of evolution is running out in Africa, and we are about to let it happen. If we let it go, this most fantastic relic of organized life on earth, no cunning can ever bring it back.''

66. Carrick, Ian. **A Right Involvement with Nature.** Frontier 13(1) February 1970: 31–33.
Compact analysis of the unity in humans and nature. Carrick urges churches to seek the aid of science and of the Bible to develop a theory of creation which will accommodate changes in the secular structure.

67. Carroll, Peter N. **Puritanism and the Wilderness: The Intellectual Significance of the New England Frontier, 1629–1700.** New York: Columbia University Press, 1969. 243 p.
A study analyzing the Puritans' complex relationship to the American wilderness and the importance of the latter in shaping thought in New England. An important conflict existed between people's desire to expand the frontier (subjugate the wilderness) and still maintain close-knit communities where Puritan religious and educational values could flourish. Selected bibliography and index.

68. Carson, Rachel L. **The Sea Around Us.** Rev. ed. New York: The New American Library, 1961. 221 p.
Representative of her many scientific and poetic writings on the oceans. This book emphasizes the origins of all life in the sea, our dependence on the waters and their inhabitants, and our obligation to preserve as well as use them. Illustrated with photographs and drawings; notes; suggested readings; and index.

69. ———. **Silent Spring.** Boston: 1962. 368 p.
A classic text which focused world attention on pesticides as an environmental hazard. Carson discusses relationships between humans and their environment in the physical world, and, in the world of thought, the relationship between science and the humanities. The final paragraph of ''Rumblings of an Avalanche'' summarizes her belief that ''Life is a miracle beyond our comprehension, and we should reverence it even when we have to struggle against it.'' The copious notes and references constitute a substantial bibliography.

70. Carvell, Fred J. and Tadlock, Max, eds. **It's Not Too Late.** Beverly Hills, Calif.: Glencoe, 1971. 312 p.
A collection of articles on the scope of our ecological concerns, on establishing priorities, and on analyzing value judgments. In the introduction the editors suggest that since the destiny of the earth and of its inhabitants is in human hands, all future actions will require planning and a high

degree of social organization and control. They warn that our imperfect knowledge may produce surprising and not always desirable results. Nevertheless, we must begin. See especially the final chapter: "The Philosophical Prelude to Environmental Change," with articles by Garrett Hardin, G. L. Kesteven, Arthur Pearl, Paul Shepard, and David C. Miller.

71. Cauthen, Kenneth. **Christian Biopolitics: A Credo and Strategy for the Future.** Nashville, Tenn.: Abingdon Press, 1971. 159 p.

After a cultural and historical analysis of human development, a theologian interprets and encourages a new consciousness both in secular society and in the churches. He calls for an alliance between thinkers of the futurist movement and church visionaries to provide the wisdom and the values to move us toward an ecologically sound and socially just world. Indexes of names and of places.

72. ———. **The Ethics of Enjoyment: . . .** Atlanta: John Knox Press, 1975. 124 p.

Essays that ask down-to-earth questions about the pursuit of happiness and what it means to be a morally responsible citizen in a confusing world. In the final chapter, Cauthen offers some solutions that should stimulate thought and discussion. Notes and bibliography.

73. Chant, Donald A., ed. **Pollution Probe.** Toronto: New Press, 1970. 209 p.

Fifteen authors from Pollution Probe, a Canadian citizens' antipollution group, express their convictions that the natural environment is being abused by industry, neglected by government, and ignored or taken for granted by vast segments of society. They explain pollution causes and environmental effects in lay terms and appeal for greater public awareness and the development of a new ecologically oriented ethic. Steps individuals may take toward achieving such an ethic are outlined.

74. Charter, S. P. R. **Man on Earth: A Preliminary Evaluation of the Ecology of Man.** Foreword by Aldous Huxley. Sausalito, Calif.: Contact Editions, 1962. 272 p.

An inquiry into some specific questions that touch moralities and philosophies affecting the lives of tomorrow's children: Will earth's natural support systems be sufficiently healthy to meet future needs? Are humans weakened by their dependence upon technology to solve problems? Will the world's heavy consumers be able to curb their greed? The role of science is central to these and other issues discussed.

75. Chaturvedi, M. D. **Wildlife Management in India.** *In*
Conservation in India: Proceedings of the Special Meeting.
New Delhi, November 24, 1965. Morges, Switzerland:
International Union for the Conservation of Nature and
Natural Resources, 1969. pp. 22–41.
An address describing wildlife distribution and management. It also emphasizes conservation as a tradition of great importance in Indian myths and folklore, in Hindu Scriptures, in the edicts of Asoka (Emperior of India, 264–227 B.C.), and in recent legislation. Chaturvedi points out the need for public understanding and concern. Bibliography.

76. Clark, Kenneth McK. **Animals and Men.** . . London:
Thames and Hudson, 1977. 240 p.
Published in support of the World Wildlife Fund. Through illustrations and descriptions of art from Western countries, Egypt, Greece, and the Near East, Clark traces conceptions that various civilizations have toward other living things. These attitudes include worship, love, admiration, fear, hatred, and now recognition of a new moral responsibility.
Adaptation by the author, Smithsonian 8(6) September 1977: 52–61.

77. Clarke, R. O. and List, P. C., eds. **Environmental**
Spectrum: . . . New York: Van Nostrand, 1974. 161 p.
Ten essays by authorities in the sciences and the humanities. They evaluate national attitudes toward economic growth, environmental quality, the human ability to "manipulate" environments, and questions of ethics and morality.

78. Clement, Roland C. **A Use for Wilderness:** . . . Audubon
Magazine 68(2) March–April 1966: 94–95.
A biologist and former vice president of the National Audubon Society summarizes the need for preserving wilderness for inspiration and spiritual regeneration, in contrast to the views of David Lowenthal and Paul Shepard, both of whom he discusses.

79. Cobb, John B. **Is It Too Late? A Theology of Ecology.**
Beverly Hills, Calif.: Bruce, 1972. 147 p.
Cobb poses his question to moral and political institutions which usually find it convenient to talk of, and do little about, their growing awareness of the ecology/population crisis. Important sections of this book include: "Non-western Views of Nature"; "Is the Subhuman World Real?"; "Christian Responsibility"; "The Philosophical Problem" (Teilhard de Chardin to Alfred North Whitehead); and "An Ecological Philosophy." Discussion questions follow each chapter; bibliography.

80. Commoner, Barry. **The Closing Circle: Nature, Man,
Technology.** New York: Knopf, 1971. 336 p.

A basic tool for those wishing to survey the essentials of "environmental crisis." Our many-faceted society must grapple with some mounting problems while seeking consensus for American economic, social, and political conduct in the coming decades. Each segment of our national life has its popular "whipping boy" who, in theory, is to blame for encouraging the huge increases in environmentally destructive capacities of agri-business and industry since World War II. Commoner maintains that economic growth is fine. "What happens to the environment is *how* the growth is achieved." See especially chapter 9, "The Technological Flaw." The book also deals with social issues and world-wide implications of ecological economies. Notes and index.

81. Conference of Modern Churchmen, 53d, Culham
College, Abingdon, Berkshire, England, July 1970. **Nature,
Man and God.** Modern Churchman 14(1) October 1970:
1–118.

Report on discussions, papers, seminars, and comments on the conference as a whole. See especially the section on "Nature"; the seminar discussion here concentrates on the teachings of Teilhard de Chardin.

82. **Conservation and Values.** The Conservation Foundation's
Thirtieth Anniversary Symposium, December 1, 1978.
Washington, D.C.: The Conservation Foundation. 72 p.

Eleven speakers and commentators presented: tributes to the founders and to the lasting goals of the Foundation; accomplishments of the environmental movement in the last thirty years; the imperatives of conservation of natural, rural, and urban areas in our present society; and a look toward the needs of the future. Conservation values, as well as pragmatic suggestions for environmental improvement, were a dominant theme. See especially William K. Reilly's "Values and the Land" and the final paper, "The Emerging Conservation Ethic," by columnist Neal R. Peirce.

83. Conservation Education Association. **Environmental
Attitudes, Ethics, Values and Their Communication.**
Syracuse: State University of New York, College of
Environmental Science and Forestry, 1974. 52 p.

Proceedings of the 21st National Conservation Education Association Conference, August 11–14, 1974. Papers (many condensed) addressing various aspects of the subject. Representatives from thirty-six states and Ontario, Canada, participated.

84. **Conservation Foundation Letter.** April and
    May 1978. 16 p.
Two letters on endangered species; each reexamines the federal government's protection program, dramatized by the snail darter-Tellico Dam
controversy. Congress is criticized for omitting ethics from its list of values
which endangered species offer the nation and the public.
    Available from the Conservation Foundation, 1717 Massachusetts Ave.,
N.W., Washington, D.C. 20036.

85. **Conservation of Nature in the Soviet Union, Some
    Problems and Solutions.** Moscow: Ministry of Agriculture of
    the USSR, 1972. 247 p.
Reports and papers to the XIth General Assembly and XIIth Technical
Meeting of the International Union for the Conservation of Nature and
Natural Resources. Several papers stress the dependence of humans on
nature; the necessity of recognizing laws of nature as the only valid basis
for regulating mutual relations; and the need for incorporating this attitude
in planning, development, education, laws, and regulations.

86. **Conservation to Aid Near East Settlement?** Environmental
    Conservation 1(1) Spring 1974: 3.
Editorial reporting conversations with individuals, urging establishment
of national parks and reserves along national boundaries. Some successful
international and bilateral conservation measures illustrate a new philosophy to preserve the common heritage.

87. **A Conversation with Frank Waters.** Interview by James
    Peterson. Psychology Today 6(12) May 1973: 63–72, 99.
A discussion of an awakening interest in ecology in North America and
the realization that ecological principles were part of Indian life. It explores
various social anomies in modern societies that have become alienated
from the spiritual side of life. This interview also touches on the psychology
of C. G. Jung. The masculine element of the Christian Church is compared
to the Pueblo Indian kiva. The women's movement and other aspects of
the modern scene are contrasted with ancient ideas such as the mystique
of the land and certain customs and educational practices of several well-
known Indian groups.

88. Coulson, C. A. **Science and Christian Belief.** London:
    Oxford University Press, 1955. 127 p.
The John Calvin McNair Lectures delivered at the University of North
Carolina at Chapel Hill in 1954. The four lectures comprise an inquiry into
the profound influence of science and the role of the scientist in the modern
world. An important objective of the lectures is to clarify Coulson's beliefs

that science's search for truth is essentially a religious activity and that humans and nature share common qualities of 'being' under God.

89. Cronin, John F. **The Social Teaching of Pope John XXIII.** Milwaukee: Bruce, 1963. 83 p.

Excerpts from the two great social encyclicals of John XXIII's pontificate: "Christianity and Social Progress" and "Peace on Earth." Concerning population imbalance, the Pope sees solutions to be found in "a renewed scientific and technical effort on man's part to deepen and extend his dominion over Nature" as among the possibilities leading to "social and economic progress."

90. Crummett, Michael S. **Stripmining: The Complete Destroyer.** IDOC Bulletin (48) October 1974: 8–10.

This article describes several groups of Native Americans whose lands, communities, traditions, and burial grounds continue to be destroyed—often by dubious procedures—by U. S. government and mining companies as they try to fill insatiable energy demands of other Americans. Nations discussed in this article are Hopi-Navajo, Cheyenne, and Crow.

91. Curry-Lindahl, Kai. **Conservation for Survival: An Ecologic Strategy.** New York: Morrow, 1972. 335 p.

A broad survey of world ecological problems. Curry-Lindahl finds it may not be too late to save us from the consequences of our own greed and mismanagement with a program for intelligent use of the earth's renewable natural resources. He employs well-documented figures and cases drawn from his career as zoologist and leader in international conservation efforts. Glossary; bibliography; index.

92. ———. **The Global Role of National Parks for the World of Tomorrow.** The Horace M. Albright Conservation Lectureship, XIV. Berkeley: University of California, School of Forestry and Conservation, 1974. 54 p.

An outline of the effects over the past one hundred years of unprecedented economic, demographic, and social growth upon some of the world's major remaining "natural areas." Many contemporary problems and challenges are touched on, with an emphasis on the need for cooperative, international planning as more important than ever to the restoration of essential ecosystems.

93. Dalton, Mary A. **The Theology of Ecology: An Interdisciplinary Concept.** Religious Education 71(1) January–February 1976: 17–26.

The article delineates Dalton's thesis that this subject would be especially apt for encouraging high school students to reevaluate the human relation to nature and to all creation. Four main themes are outlined: the theology of ecology; a theology of nature; man's unity with nature; a new restraint toward what we seek to acquire or consume and toward the types of pleasures we indulge in. Notes.

94. Dansereau, Pierre. **Inscape and Landscape: The Human Perception of Environment.** New York: Columbia University Press, 1975. 124 p.

"The environmental disorder which we face at this time is the result of the discrepancy between man's intentions and his achievements." The human's selective perception of his world guides his reshaping of the landscape. Ways to acquire the needed knowledge and vision are reviewed, and means of planning and shaping the environment are shown. A philosophy to achieve the "joyous austerity" is seen as essential. Examples draw on Dansereau's experience as a botanist, ecologist, and Canadian. Bibliography.

Darling, Frank Fraser: see Fraser Darling, Frank

95. Dasmann, Raymond F. **The Conservation Alternative.** New York: Wiley, 1975. 164 p.

Most of the book is devoted to discussions of specific environmental problems and their solutions. The latter are based on the conservation principle, which includes recognition of the right of all species to continue to inherit the earth. There are occasional references to particular religions, e.g., attributing the growth of technology to Christianity and Islam (p. 100). Bibliographical notes at the end of each chapter.

96. ———. **Conservation, Counter-Culture and Separate Realities.** Environmental Conservation 1(2) Summer 1974: 133–137.

An ecologist examines the literature on the social phenomena of the 1960s. From the renewal of interest in religion Dasmann finds an outgrowth that has a "potential for major changes in human attitudes toward nature conservation." References.

97. Davies, Brian. **Seal Song.** New York: Viking, 1978. 93 p.

The life (and death) of the harp seal, written by a Canadian who is executive director of the International Fund for Animal Welfare. The descriptive text includes accounts of the annual hunts of these seals and their pups for the luxury fur-coat market. These mammals and other marine species are doubly endangered as their environment becomes polluted by industrial and agricultural poisons, causing natural food supplies to disappear. The epilogue is an appeal to humanity to recognize the common grounds we share with other animals. Color photographs by Eliot Porter.

33

98. Deloria, Vine. **God Is Red.** New York: Grosset,
   1973. 376 p.
A study comparing some Christian doctrines and beliefs with those associated with American Indian tribal groups; discussed are origins, developments, influences, and decline of religions. In chapter 16, Deloria states that many tribal concepts are applicable to modern religious and environmental quandaries.

99. Derr, Thomas S. **Religion's Responsibility for the
   Ecological Crisis; an Argument Run Amok.** Worldview 18(1)
   January 1975: 39–45.
At head of title: Lynn White and his magical essay. To Lynn White is usually attributed the thesis that some Judeo-Christian doctrines are responsible for degredation of the environment. Derr claims that White has been misunderstood, as such an idea is contrary to White's usual teachings.

100. Derrick, Christopher. **The Delicate Creation: Towards a
   Theology of the Environment.** Foreword by René Dubos;
   introduction by John Cardinal Wright. Old Greenwich,
   Conn.: Devin-Adair, 1972. 129 p.
Derrick criticizes and rejects both materialism and Manichaeism; he sees them as the twin dangers in our attitudes. His solution is to develop a sense of reverence for all life, a "cosmic piety" based on Catholic principles. Some of his conclusions, especially concerning population control, may be startling and seem impractical. Nevertheless, they are, to him, logical outgrowths of his premise.

101. De Wolf, L. Harold. **Responsible Freedom: Guidelines to
   Christian Action.** New York: Harper, 1971. 366 p.
Chapter 11 of this comprehensive treatment of Christian ethics deals with our natural environment. It outlines the urgency of the problem, distinguishes basic threats, discusses biblical views on the natural environment, and suggests guidelines for conservation measures. Indexes of names and topics.

102. **Dimensions of the Future: The Spirituality of Teilhard de
   Chardin.** Edited by Marvin Kessler and Bernard Brown.
   Washington, D.C.: Corpus Books, 1968. 216 p.
A collection of papers (mostly by theologians) from a conference held in 1966 at St. Mary's College, Kansas. Pertinent passages discuss Teilhard's thoughts and observations regarding human understanding and cosmic evolution. Notes on contributors; index.

103. Disch, Robert, ed. **The Ecological Conscience: Values for Survival.** Englewood Cliffs, N.J.: Prentice-Hall, 1970. 206 p.

An anthology of sixteen essays which together underscore the profound change that industrialized nations will have to undergo if they are to alter the values and attitudes they hold toward the natural world. New ethics, based on the insights of ecology, must affect the policies and practices of science and technology, of politics and economics. Contributors range from well-known authorities like Barry Commoner, Paul Ehrlich, Ian McHarg, and Aldo Leopold to social critics such as Lewis Mumford, Paul Goodman, and Lawrence Slobodkin. The more esoteric problems are explored by Thomas Merton, Buckminster Fuller, Allan Watts, and Gary Snyder.

104. Ditmanson, Harold H. **The Call for a Theology of Creation.** Dialog 3(4) Autumn 1964: 264–273.

Ditmanson, a professor of theology, examines the views of Charles Raven, Joseph Sittler, Edmund Schlink, and others to discover why the biblical attitude toward nature, originally affirmative, has been abandoned and degraded by churches. He then presents his own interpretation of the creation; it includes all nature which has its own significance and permanent place in the purpose of God. Bibliographic notes.

105. Dobzhansky, Theodosius. **Teilhard de Chardin and the Orientation of Evolution: A Critical Essay.** Zygon 3(3) September 1968: 242–258.

Dobzhansky uses the word criticism to mean "a reasoned opinion of. . . ." He believes with Teilhard that both knowledge gained from science (plus inspiration of poets, artists, and mystics) and religious experience are necessary to human life. The latter is not provable—as is scientific theory—but it is not contradictory to scientific fact. Such an experience can be, and in Teilhard is, synthesized.

106. Dodson Gray, Elizabeth. **Energy Oratorio,** Wellesley, Mass.: Gray, 1978. 19 p.

Part 1 tells the story of evolution as God's continuing creation of the world and how it is a gift which belongs equally to all. Parts 2–3 describe the laying down of energy (coal, oil, and gas) and its exploitation by humans who did not count the cost. Parts 4–5 redefine "neighbor" to include future generations of humans and all creation. Finally, there is a prayer for ecological justice inspired by Christ's teachings.

Available from NCCC Energy Project, 475 Riverside Drive (Room 572), New York, N.Y. 10027.

107. Donaldson, James. **America the Beautiful:**
Interdependence with Nature. Foundations 19(3)
July–September 1976: 238–256 and **Response** by Virginia
Carney, 252–253, and by Glenn D. Hammer, 254–256.

Donaldson seeks a new vision of interdependence based on Christian (his
religion) American Indian culture (his heritage) and concern for the environment. After analyzing the troubles of today's world, he describes the
good life as lived in his community in the Methow Valley of Washington
State. Carney, a conservationist, states that the churches and the environmentalists need to retrace their thinking back to original beliefs in the
dignity of humans and respect for all life and go forward again from there.
Hammer, a theologian, doubts the feasibility of Donaldson's way of life,
but agrees with his emphasis on the need for a "new" theology in
Christianity.

108. Dorst, Jean. **Before Nature Dies.** Translated [from the
French] by Constance B. Sherman. Boston: Houghton, 1970.
352 p.

Before we can apply either moral or material solutions to the present
adversary state between human societies and nature, we must clearly
understand the impact of those societies on the earth. Dorst reviews this
from earliest times and on a worldwide basis, studying mankind as both
ravager and defender of nature. Our spiritual as well as physical need for
a sound environmental ethic is stressed. Preface by Prince Bernhard.
Color plates; black and white photographs; drawings; bibliography; index.

109. Douglas, William O. **The Three Hundred Year War: A
Chronicle of Ecological Disaster.** New York: Random House,
1972. 215 p.

An eminent jurist and conservationist traces the history of the "war" in
the destruction of America's wilderness, from the earliest settlers to its
culmination in the age of technology. He maintains that the survival of
humanity and of the biosphere depends on a spiritual awakening of the
American people and their development of an aggressive but responsible
citizen action. Laws alone are inadequate to avoid ecological disaster.

110. Dubos, René. **A God Within:** . . . New York: Scribner,
1972. 325 p.

Taking a fresh look at the external world, the "spirit" of places, and the
"spirit" or "god" within each of us, this optimistic scientist writes that
we can reverse the destructive trends of recent times and strive for a
healthy environment. This "eleventh commandment" should encompass
both the external world and the quality of human life within it. Dubos
makes the point that environments can and do survive extreme upsets;
they evolve, and the resulting changes may be effected best by the

Benedictine tradition of practical and theoretical stewardship, accompanied by reverence. A reprint of the latter position may be found in Psychology Today 6(12) May 1973: 54–60. Extensive notes and bibliography.

111. ———. **Life is an Endless Give-and-Take with Earth and All Her Creatures.** Smithsonian 1(1) April 1970: 8–17.
The Smithsonian Institution launched its magazine with this lead article highlighting some of the interrelationships found in various natural cycles. The worst of the human intrusions upon a healthy earth are amusingly illustrated by artist John Osborn.

112. ———. **Reason Awake: Science for Man.** New York: Columbia University Press, 1970. 280 p.
A critique of science and scientific technology based on lectures for the Institute for the Study of Science in Human Affairs. The foreword sums up Dubos' hope that science may help shape the future by providing sufficient knowledge of the cosmos and of human nature. He believes that when we really enter the age of science, we will give up crude attempts at domination and will instead learn to live in harmony with nature.

113. Dumoulin, Heinrich, ed. **Buddhism in the Modern World.** New York: Macmillan, 1976. 368 p.
See especially "Principles of Ethics" (pp. 25–30), which includes statements on the origin and meaning of humanity and our relations with other creatures. Bibliography and index.

114. Dunn, James M., Loring, Ben E., and Strickland, Phil D. **Endangered Species.** Nashville, Tenn.: Broadman Press, 1976. 153 p.
A concise book designed to contribute to public education on world hunger needs and to show Christians how personal and institutional action can relieve hunger problems threatening so much of humanity. Chapter 7, "The Earth is the Lord's—or is It?" describes the increasingly evident interrelatedness of earth's natural ecosystems. It summarizes the main challenges, especially for people in developed countries, to coping with the complicated effects of consumerism, overpopulation, and the destruction of food systems. Biblical citations from Old and New Testaments. Appendixes; notes; bibliography.

115. Durrell, Gerald. **The Stationary Ark.** New York: Simon, 1976. 159 p.
This is one of many funny, wise, and informative books by this writer. It is representative of the philosophy that led him to establish the Jersey Wildlife Preservation Trust (a breeding zoo for endangered species) and the Wildlife Trust International, its overseas arm. He believes that all

creatures have the right to exist—not for our benefit but because they are a part of the totality of life.

116. Eco-catastrophe. By the Editors of Ramparts. New York: Harper and Row, 1970. 158 p.

Selected articles which articulate a "radical perspective" of environmental crisis in American society and the exploitative attitudes responsible for much of it. Chapters pertain to corporate power structure, international business, natural resources and industrial pollution, the bureaucratic establishment, and other subjects. Illustrations.

● 117. **The Ecologist** 4(9) November 1974: 313–349 and **Resurgence** 5(5) November–December 1974: 1–37. Joint issue.

A collection of articles and book reviews on various religions and beliefs which provide spiritual guidance toward stable living in harmony with the natural world and with other people. Some of these are the basic beliefs of several African peoples, Zen, "radical" Christianity, Sufism, and Hinduism.

118. **Ecology.** Bioscience 14(7) July 1964: 9–41.

Contributors to this special issue raise grave questions on the state of the human environment and suggest that the responsibility of scientists—particularly biologists and ecologists—is to revise and extend their thinking on these basic questions. Principal articles by Paul B. Sears, Eugene P. Odum, W. Frank Blair, Pierre Dansereau, John F. Reed, Lamont C. Cole, and Edward S. Deevy.

119. **Ecology and Justice.** Foundations (A Baptist Journal of History and Theology) 17(2) April–June 1974: 99–172.

A collection of articles on "eco justice," defined in the lead editorial as the "interrelationship between social justice and environmental quality." Partial contents: "Theological Meaning of Eco-justice Through Institutional Change," by Jitsuo Morikawa; "Salvation and Ecology: Missionary Imperatives in Light of a New Cosmology," by Owen D. Owens; "Eco-justice: Challenge to the Churches in the 1970's," by Norman J. Faramelli; "Ecological Wholeness and Justice: The Imperative of God," by Board of National Ministries Staff; "Ancient Priests and Modern Polluters," by Phyllis Trible; "The Local Church and the Environmental Crisis," by John B. Cobb.

120. **Ecology and Religion Newsletter.** Edited by Dennis G. Kuby. 1+ November 1973+ Berkeley, Calif.: Ministry of Ecology. Monthly except July and August.

Articles, news briefs, and humor for an interfaith network linking ecology and religion. Available from the Ministry of Ecology, P. O. Box 1251, Berkeley, Calif. 94704.

For a description of the work of the Ministry of Ecology, see Catalyst for Environmental Quality 5(3) Fall 1976: 15–16.

121. **Ecology and the Church.** Review and Expositor 69(1) Winter 1972: 3–76.

An entire issue devoted to Baptist views on the theme, with articles by theologians and others in varied professions. Contributors include: Wayne H. Davis, Eric C. Rust, Henlee H. Barnette, Gaylord A. Nelson, Victor C. Ferkiss, Alan F. Guttmacher, and William P. Tuch.

122. Edberg, Rolf. **On the Shred of a Cloud: Notes in a Travel Book.** Translated [from the Swedish] by Sven Ahman. University: University of Alabama Press, 1969. 200 p.

A Swedish provincial governor muses on the beauties of nature and the dangers confronting it through human error or intent. The final chapter asks if the next generation will have what previous ones have not—the wisdom and courage to develop a new philosophy of relationships between people and nature and the institutions to fulfill such a philosophy. Bibliographical notes.

123. Ehrenfeld, David. **The Arrogance of Humanism.** New York: Oxford University Press, 1978. 286 p.

Contemporary humanism, in Ehrenfeld's view, is a destructive force practiced unpremeditatively but universally with virtually the zeal of a religion. Such humanism encourages supreme faith in human reason to rearrange the world of nature and to direct our present and our future in any way we see fit. In developing his thesis Ehrenfeld presents an analysis of assumptions of current philosophies and their relationship to reality. He discusses the fallacies of the current insistence on evaluating everything in monetary and economic terms and of seeking solutions to problems through sheer accumulation of statistics. Environmentalists, in assessing the immediate economic values of nature, are not exempt from the arrogance of humanism.

124. Ehrlich, Paul R. **Ecologists, Ethics, and the Environment.** BioScience 27(4) April 1977: 239.

A population expert asks the vexing ethical questions that apply to world dilemmas of population, environment, and resources.

125. Eiseley, Loren C. **The Invisible Pyramid.** New York: Scribner, 1970. 173 p.

Philosophical essays by an anthropologist whose familiarity with expired civilizations leads him to examine the nature of man in the modern world of machines and cities. He speculates about ancient human aspirations and about modern ones which ignore or exploit nature as well as our own natural beings. He believes we must develop a perceptive and sympathetic—rather than adversary—relationship with our fellow creatures.

126. ———. **Man: The Lethal Factor.** American Scientist
    51(1) March 1963: 71–83.
The Phi Beta Kappa-Sigma Xi Lecture given in December 1962 at the University of Pennsylvania, Philadelphia. Since ancient times, man the wanderer has perceived himself as both part of and apart from nature. Though humans devise laws and cultural forms to control nature, we must learn that, in the final analysis, the human race is subject to natural laws. Eiseley touches on the arrogance of much in modern science and technology, such as the arms race. He suggests that only religion's most profound images may be powerful enough to turn us away from annihilation and toward creation.

127. Ekirch, Arthur A. **Man and Nature in America.** New
    York: Columbia University Press, 1963. 233 p.
The American experience of changing an almost untouched wilderness into a highly industrialized land whose resources are fast diminishing, all in less than 400 years, has given us special vantage for comprehending the power humans have to alter the earth. The evolution of American attitudes to nature is traced from the colonial thinkers to those of modern times. Notes and index.

128. Elder, Frederick. **Crisis in Eden: A Religious Study of
    Man and Environment.** New York: Abingdon, 1970. 172 p.
A study of two contrasting schools of environmental thought: the "inclusionist," which espouses a holistic approach to the human position in the natural order, and "exclusionists," which holds that humans stand apart from nature and are superior to it. The theological and social differences between these positions are the foci of most efforts to reach ethical judgments on short- and long-range decisions regarding the environment. In concluding, Elder suggests one approach to the crisis may lie in a new, activist asceticism which emphasizes restraint, the quality of existence, and reverence for life, and that the responsibility for rediscovering the theme of man-nature harmony lies with the churches. Extensive bibliography and index.

129. Elwood, Douglas J. **Primitivism or Technocracy: Must
    We Choose?** Christian Century 88(48) December 1, 1971:
    1413–1418.
Summarizes the views toward nature of primitive peoples, Asian religions, and technologists and concludes that there is much untapped wisdom

among Christian thinkers to indicate that our reunion with both nature and God is possible.

130. Emmel, Thomas C., ed. **Global Perspectives on Ecology.**
Palo Alto, Calif.: Mayfield, 1977. 522 p.
A collection of reprints of articles from journals and excerpts from books. Grouped in three sections: Basic ecological principles and the effect of human activity on ecosystems; "Case-studies of Environmental Disruptions Throughout the World and Possible Remedial Actions"; and "The Future." Each contains many references to the ethics, philosophy, or cultural background on which actions may be based. An editor's introduction prefaces each section; bibliographic notes end each chapter. Indexes.

131. Engel, David E. **Elements in a Theology of Environment.**
Zygon 5(3) September 1970: 216–228.
A lecture given to Pittsburgh Theological Seminary's continuing education program in 1970. Engel studies the Judeo-Christian biblical tradition which, he says, clearly gives man dominion over the earth. He discusses the arguments of Lynn White and Ian L. McHarg. He concludes that the history of human violence toward earth reveals the necessity of developing an ethic of nature that equals traditional human-centered models of theology. Notes.

132. **Environment and Americans: The Problem of Priorities.**
Edited by Roderick Nash. New York: Holt, 1972. 119 p.
A collection of articles that provides a concise history of and introduction to the subject. "The Pioneer Perspective" is followed by "Varieties of Conservation" and "The Ecological Perspective." The writers are specialists from many disciplines. Suggestions for further reading.

133. **The Environmental Crisis.** Christian Century 87(40)
October 7, 1970: 1174–1196.
The entire issue is devoted to the environmental crisis, with pertinent articles by Ian G. Barbour, John B. Cobb, Donald E. Gowan, Thomas K. Kearn, and William R. Hoyt ("Zen Buddhism and Western Alienation from Nature").

134. **The Environmental Crisis.** Edited by Harold W.
Helfrich. New Haven: Yale University Press, 1970–71. 2 v.
Volume 1: Man's Struggle to Live with Himself, 187 p.;
Volume 2: Agenda for Survival, 234 p.
These volumes consist of lectures comprising a 1968–69 symposium on "Issues in Environmental Crisis" at the Yale University School of Forestry. Many subjects are covered in the hope of teaching the interre-

latedness of all life and of helping to bridge information gaps between humanists, environmental scientists, governments, and a concerned public. Bibliographic references.

135. **Environmental Ethics.** 1(1)+ Spring 1979+
Albuquerque, N.M.: The John Muir Institute for
Environmental Studies and the University of New Mexico.
Quarterly.

The first journal in this country to cover the philosophical aspects of environmental problems. Interdisciplinary in approach, it aims to bring together the environmental interests of philosophers with the concerns of ecologists. Each issue contains scholarly articles by experts, book reviews, short news, and notes on current developments in the field.

136. **Ethics for Environment: Three Religious Strategies.**
Edited by Dave Steffenson, Walter J. Herscher, and Robert
S. Cook. Green Bay, Wisc.: Green Bay Ecumenical Center,
1973. 132 p.

Proceedings of a national conference held at the University of Wisconsin-Green Bay, June 11–13, 1973. As indicated in the introduction, the talks and discussions focus on 1) contributions from Judeo-Christian, Eastern-Mystical, and Native American thought; 2) a practical example in land-use ethics; and 3) an attempt to synthesize and integrate "a religiously based approach to land use" and other factors in the environment. Participants include George A. Maloney; H. Paul Santmire; Rajagopal Ryali; J. W. E. Newberry; and Robert Florence. Notes at the end of each section; bibliography.

137. **Faith, Science and the Future.** Geneva, Switzerland:
Church and Society, World Council of Churches, 1978.
236 p.

Preparatory readings for a world conference organized by the World Council of Churches at the Massachusetts Institute of Technology, Cambridge, Mass., July 12–24, 1979. A pre-conference summary of the major questions to be asked and debated concerning the future development of just and "sustainable societies" in the world. Chapter 5, "Rethinking the Criteria for Quality of Life," establishes some of the parameters addressed throughout the book: ethical commitments, energy, resources, the churches and nuclear energy, what is a "sustainable society," appropriate technology, and the need to protect nature now that we are clearly in a position to destroy her if we do not change our ways.

Resolutions approved by the Conference will be published.

138. Ferkiss, Victor. **The Future of Technological**
Civilization. New York: Braziller, 1974. 369 p.

A study to develop the basis of a value-system that will enable us "to deal effectively with the humanity-technology-nature relationships'' of the future. Ferkiss posits that in the twenty-first century, *communication,* not production ''will be the prime function of technology, and the social impact of technology will be even greater than it is today.'' Historical, liberal ideologies espousing individualism (as opposed to state management of economies) are outmoded; instead he proposes a new philosophy, ''ecological humanism.'' Chapters 18 and 19 describe how this idea may restore humanity to its proper role in a balanced planetary ecosystem and within a world political system. Notes; bibliography; index.

139. Finnerty, Adam D. **No More Plastic Jesus: Global Justice and Christian Lifestyle.** Maryknoll, N.Y.: Orbis, 1977. 223 p.

The philosophy of this book may be found in understanding what Finnerty and others in the Simple Living movement mean by ''creative simplicity.'' It is based upon the idea that early Christian teachings may be applied to modern needs. Principal among these is the search for ways of living that limit prodigious consumption and waste. Appendixes; bibliography; periodicals; films and audio-visual materials.

140. Fire, John and Erdoes, Richard. **Lame Deer, Seeker of Visions.** New York: Simon, 1972. 188 p.

Autobiography of a modern medicine man and great-grandson of the first Lame Deer known to the white conquerors of America. Some passages, illustrations, and the last chapter in particular, set forth his belief in the oneness of the universe.

141. Flader, Susan L. **Thinking Like a Mountain; Aldo Leopold and the Evolution of an Ecological Attitude Toward Deer, Wolves and Forests.** Columbia: University of Missouri Press, 1974. 284 p.

Flader analyzes the development of Leopold's thought and changing attitudes toward the intellectual problem of deer-wolf-forestry interrelationships. There is a biographical sketch of his professional career and an analysis of the development of his philosophy, placed in the broader context of historical events in the ecological movement. A sympathetic case study of Aldo Leopold.

142. Fosburgh, Pieter W. **The Natural Thing: The Land and Its Citizens.** New York: MacMillan, 1959. 255 p.

A collection of essays on places in New York State which illustrate conservation practices or their lack. His definition of conservation as concerned with the human spiritual, mental, and material needs is outlined in the introduction.

143. Fox, Michael W. **Between Animal and Man.** New York: Coward, 1976. 223 p.

A veterinarian and expert on ethology introduces the reader to a study of similarities and differences among human beings and between humans and animals. Through understanding and knowledge, he hopes people will redevelop reverence for all life and express it in actions that benefit present and future generations. Photographs and drawings; charts.

144. Fraser Darling, Frank. **Wilderness and Plenty.** Introduction by Paul Brooks. Boston: Houghton, 1970. 84 p.

The Reith lectures, delivered for the BBC in 1969, are a mini-course in the essential ecological/environmental realities of our time. Fraser Darling is not a pessimist, but as a scientist he sounds a warning to governments and citizens to become informed about the long-term global effects of short-term, politically expedient policies. He concludes with a vision of our obligation toward Earth in the form of an amalgamation of several ethics: 1) that nature is worthy of respect and protection in her own right; 2) human sexuality responsibility; and 3) a land ethic. Together these comprise a "philosophy of restraint" based on love and civility. References.

145. —— and Milton, John P., eds. **Future Environments of North America.** Garden City, N.Y.: Natural History Press, 1966. 76 p.

From a conference convened by the Conservation Foundation in April 1965 at Airlie House, Warrenton, Va. Edited papers and discussion. Many refer to philosophical and religious principles. Clarence Glacken's "Reflections on the Man-Nature Theme as a Subject for Study" (a brief review of human concepts and values as expressed in literature) and Pierre Dansereau's section on cultural values in "Ecological Impact and Human Ecology" are examples. Each paper has bibliographical notes.

146. Freudenstein, Eric G. **Ecology and the Jewish Tradition.** Judaism 19(4) Fall 1970: 406–414.

A chemist by profession, Freudenstein is also learned in Judaism. He cites scholars and texts which demonstrate the Jews' concern for the environment from the earliest times. He indicates that Israel, with its high regard for public welfare, land reclamation, and general awareness of the importance of ecology, is an example of this ancient message in action.

147. Frith, Harold J. **Wildlife Conservation.** Sydney: Angus and Robertson, 1973. 414 p.

In his introduction Frith points out that the initial hue and cry over "the environment" was human centered—polluted cities, overconsumption, etc. However, this is changing, and Australians have in recent years devoted skills and money to solving the plight of their wildlife. The study includes wildlife habitats, acclimation, hunting, commercialization, endangered fauna, and management. Extensive bibliography; index; maps; figures; black and white photographs.

148. Frome, Michael. **The Story of Conservation Stretches Back to Our Land's Early Inhabitants.** Smithsonian 1(12) March 1971, 16–27.

A summary of some American attitudes toward nature. These include Native Americans and a few far-sighted white leaders.

149. Gardner, John F. **The Environmental Crisis.** Proceedings, The Myrin Institute for Adult Education (24) Spring 1971: 23–39.

Gardner answers his own questions on the subject as if posed by an imaginary interlocutor. He seems cautiously optimistic that people can be educated to cultivate intuitive forms of thought that encourage care for, and recognition of, nature for her own sake and that shift away from self-centered human activities.

150. Gibson, William E. **Eco Justice: Burning Word: Heilbroner and Jeremiah to the Church.** Foundations 20(4) October–December 1977, 318–327. **Critique** by Peter J. Gomes, 329–332.

Two diverging views are represented in this article and in its critique. Gibson believes that the world is God's creation and that it behooves humans to live with justice toward all beings, thus establishing "ecological harmony or balance in the context of social justice." For the biblical concept of stewardship, he quotes Jeremiah. For a recent assessment, he turns to Robert Heilbroner's "An Inquiry into the Human Prospect." Finally, he challenges the church to provide the vision and leadership toward that transformation.

Gomes, a Professor of Christian Morals, thinks Gibson's role for the church is too modest and gives his own suggestions for Christian living. His thinking is based, however, on a view opposite to that of Gibson, namely that the Judeo-Christian religions are hostile to nature and that Christians are less concerned with this world than with the hereafter.

151. Glacken, Clarence J. **Traces on the Rhodian Shore. . .** Berkeley: University of California Press, 1967. 76 p.

A scholarly work of great scope, largely based on original sources, with citations and footnotes. Glacken investigates Western thought from ancient times to the end of the eighteenth century. The awesome questions of the human relation to earth and to God—the purposes of life, man's power over much in nature, as well as nature's "indifference" and seeming lack of design—were of as much concern to the thinkers of the earliest agricultural civilizations as they are today. Bibliography and index.

152. Glass, Hiram B. **Science and Ethical Values.** Chapel
Hill: University of North Carolina Press, 1965. 101 p.
Three essays delivered as the John Calvin McNair lectures (1965) on
relations between science and morals. The first discourse traces the origin
of human ethics to biological evolution and studies conflicts in values,
past, present, and future. The second deals with ethics and genetic manipulation. The final lecture examines the philosophy of science and the
need to relate science to ethics.

153. Goodman, Daniel. **Ideology and Ecological Irrationality.**
BioScience 20(23) December 1970: 1247–1252.
A zoologist writes that existing ideologies are moving us toward ecological
catastrophe. He urges measures to educate both the public and government
at all levels to political responsibility if we are to achieve stable societies
in healthy environments.

154. **The Gospel of Ecology.** *In* The American Environment.
2d ed. Edited by Roderick Nash. New York: Addison-
Wesley, 1968. pp. 225–348.
The Gospel of Ecology outlines the changes in attitudes and values which
produced the intensity of environmental concerns in 1969–70.

155. Gowan, Donald E. and Schumaker, Millard. **Genesis
and Ecology: An Exchange.** Kingston, Ontario: Queen's
Theological College, 1973. 31 p.
A vigorous debate between two theologians on the claim that biblical
views permit and encourage humans to assume the freedom to manipulate
the environment for their own benefit regardless of the "rights" of the
rest of life.

156. Graham, Frank. **Man's Dominion: the Story of
Conservation in America.** Drawings by John Pimlott. New
York: M. Evans; and distributed by Lippincott, 1971. 346 p.
Written for the non-specialist, this book traces the origins of today's
conservation issues and attitudes from the mid-1880s until the passage of
The Wilderness Act in 1964. It then looks to the future in two chapters,
"The Spirit" and "The Flesh," probing ethical values involved in the
preservation of wilderness and in the direct threats to our physical well-
being in environmental contamination. As much as possible, the story is
told through the words of the original conservationists. Notes.

157. Graves, John. **Goodbye to a River.** New York: Knopf,
1960. 306 p.
This narrative about the Brazos River country in Texas is by a man who
knew miles of it well in childhood and who returned there in later life at

a time when the Brazos was threatened with more dams. The author mingles its history, lore, and adventure with his personal quest to absorb and write of the meaning of the place. He writes of the value of acquaintanceship with the land, the human beings, and the wildlife that are a part of a region where scraping a living is not easy. He deals with life's inevitable changes; with life styles; hunting; and the need all creatures have for the perpetuation of quiet places, existing naturally. Bibliography.

158. Green, Timothy. **Richard Adams' Long Journey from "Watership Down."** With photographs by Peter Hirst-Smith. Smithsonian 10(4) July 1979: 76–83.
An introduction to the life and work of a contemporary novelist. In his activities and his writing, Adams lives his belief in the need for care and protection of animals. He dreams of worldwide efforts to carry out these aims.

159. Greer, Mildred P. **Nature and Morality: Consideration of Natural Grounds for a System of Ethics.** Ph.D. dissertation, Syracuse University, 1973. 236 p.
Greer defines homeostasis as the basic principle of life, encompassing interdependency, diversity, death, and renewal. In a homeostatic society God is the force around which the whole society is organized and harmoniously integrated. The Hopi Indians and the Inuit Eskimos of Unalkleet are examples of such societies. Western culture is a force that threatens to destory these and other societies. Bibliography.
Abstract in "Dissertation Abstracts International."

160. Hahn, Emily. **A Reporter at Large: Getting Through to the Others.** The New Yorker 54(10), April 24, 1978: 42–90.
Includes an interview with Michael W. Fox, Director of the Humane Society's Institute for the Study of Animal Problems. Fox's writing and work in animal communication are aimed at instilling in humans greater understanding and respect for all life.

161. Halle, Louis J. **Spring in Washington.** Foreword by Roger T. Peterson. Drawings by Frances L. Jacques. New York: Harper, 1947. 234 p.
This nature classic portrays the annual rebirth of the countryside in and near Washington, D.C., and relates these day-to-day observations to eternal values. Halle pleads for seeing nature, including human nature, as a whole rather than through the narrow focus of overspecialization.

162. Hamilton, David R. L. **Technology, Man and Environment.** New York: Scribner, 1973. 357 p.
A fairly detailed account for the layman of the accomplishments of tech-

nology. These are judged against a background of what recent developments are doing to the natural environment. In chapter 13, "Technology and the Planet," Hamilton discusses these effects in some detail. In the final chapter, "Guiding Technology," he reviews some of the measures—which must be based on new attitudes and values—for regulating technology.

163. Hamilton, Michael, ed. **This Little Planet.** New York: Scribner, 1970. 241 p.

Collection of essays by scientists, outlining problems of population, scarcity, and conservation; with reponses by Christian theologians also knowledgeable in science. The religious essays, particularly, indicate the need for ethical considerations in political and social decisions involving these problems. See especially "Biblical Roots of an Ecological Conscience," by Conrad Bonifazi.

164. Hammerton, H. J. **Unity of Creation in the Apocalypse.** Church Quarterly Review, January–March 1967: 20–33.

A persuasive account of the high status of animals in God's grace; of their degradation in theology from the Middle Ages to recent times; of the destruction of the natural world as described by Rachel Carson; and the promise of balance, peace, and love in the Apocalypse.

165. Hampton, H. Duane. **Counter Trends in the History of Conservation.** Western Highlands 5(3) Spring 1979: 10–14.

Conservation in America reflects both the aesthetic and the utilitarian views. The latter has dominated, supported by the "myth of superabundance" and growing industrial efficiency. The works of George P. Marsh in the mid-nineteenth century first alerted the national conscience to the dangers of continued exploitation. Hampton believes attitudes can and do change and he writes it is urgent to educate the public that aesthetic and utilitarian principles are compatible with the land ethic of Aldo Leopold.

166. Hanley, Wayne. **Natural History in America: From Mark Catesby to Rachel Carson.** New York: Published for Massachusetts Audubon Society by Quadrangle/New York Times Book, 1977. 344 p.

Changing views of nature in America from the early eighteenth century to the twentieth are shown, largely through the writings of the leading naturalists and their life stories. Color plates; black and white drawings.

167. Hardin, Garrett. **Exploring New Ethics for Survival: The Voyage of Spaceship Beagle.** New York: Viking, 1972. 273 p.

Using a fable within a science-fiction framework, Hardin expounds on the population-environmental-quality-of-life complexities and advocates radical alternatives to our lifestyle. Spaceship Beagle searches for habitable planets in other solar systems some two hundred years hence. Man by then has exhausted the capacity of earth to support his numbers and demands. Ironically, the ethical misconceptions that despoiled earth continue in the spaceship.

168. —— and Baden, John, eds. **Managing the Commons.** San Francisco: Freeman, 1977. 294 p.

This collection of essays by the editors and other contributors opens a discussion on how best to improve human welfare without deleterious environmental effects. The writers assume that "unmanaged commons" can no longer be tolerated. In an essay "The Tragedy of the Commons," Hardin announces the "principle of competitive exclusion"—over-use and crowding results in destruction of common resources and, therefore, no one has their use. We must relinquish some of our freedoms if we are to avoid this catastrophe.

169. Harrison, Gordon A. **Earthkeeping: The War with Nature and a Proposal for Peace.** Boston: Houghton, 1971. 176 p.

A sharp criticism of our economic, political, and value systems as the cause of environmental degradation. Improvement must come through conservation measures and environmental management, based on revised value judgments. An individual sense of responsibility and citizen action can change our outlook and, eventually, our systems.

170. Harshbarger, Luther H. and Mourant, John A. **Judaism and Christianity: Perspectives and Traditions.** Boston: Allyn and Bacon, 1968. 480 p.

A survey of basic issues and ideas historically associated with Judeo-Christian traditions, including shared backgrounds, divergent paths, and beliefs. Written for college use and to give information to persons seeking to strengthen inter-faith cooperation. See especially "A Mythological Scientific Inference: The Fall of Nature" and "The Principle of Plenitude," which reveal that both faiths have reproached believers for their self-centered views.

171. Harvey, Brian and Hallett, John D. **Environment and Society: an Introductory Analysis.** London: Macmillan, 1977. 163 p.

A textbook for undergraduate, multidisciplinary studies of environmental problems. There are brief chapters on basic ecology and the development of the environmental issue. Other chapters examine bases and beliefs underlying possible solutions to environmental problems. The final chapters ask questions concerning the course of the future, and the role of technology, the humanities, and social institutions.

172. Hatch, Robert McC. **Cornerstones for a Conservation Ethic.** Atlantic Naturalist 12(4) April–June 1957: 154–158.
In this speech to the twenty-second North American Wildlife Conference, Hatch says that conservation is a "spiritual cause, grounded in the Bible." The cornerstones of a conservation ethic include foresight involving the ethical relationship between generations, vision that sees beyond economics, and reverence in place of destruction.

173. Heal, Fred. **Keeping the Options Open.** Journal of Environmental Education 5(2) Winter 1973: 23–27.
A brief review of the destruction of ecological diversity by modern technology, followed by various writers' opinions of its impact on life on this planet. References.

174. Hefner, Philip J. **Toward a New Doctrine of Man: The Relationship of Man and Nature.** Zygon 2(2) June 1967: 127–151.
Paper by a professor of systematic theology to the University of Chicago's Divinity School centennial conference in 1966. Hefner elaborates on themes stressing the significance of humans' inseparability from social and cultural influences. These themes imply that people are of greater matter and influence than natural environments. He discusses the "spiritual or psychic" dimension, or what Teilhard called the "Noosphere" of life ("matter, life, thought, society," part of cosmic evolutionary struggle in which the potentially possible becomes real in the universe). Hefner concludes that people have an obligation to control more intelligently the natural world that is subject to us. Based on this conclusion, and with guidance from Christian principles, he offers proposals for a "Doctrine of Man." Bibliographic notes.
   This paper is included in "The Future of Empirical Theology," Bernard E. Meland, ed., Chicago: University of Chicago Press, 1969.

175. Heilbroner, Robert L. **An Inquiry into the Human Prospect.** New York: Norton, 1974. 150 p.
Five essays of reflections on our anxious age. The first sets forth the dimensions of real and attitudinal changes in modern American society. Those following cover major external challenges, such as the consequences of population explosion; "socio-economic capabilities for response"; speculations on human nature; and the "political dimension." Final thoughts are on the likelihood of a gradual, sweeping alteration of many of our present economic and political institutions.

176. ———. **Second Thoughts on 'The Human Prospect.'**
Futures 7(1) February 1975, 31–40.
This article was written fifteen months after publication of "The Human Prospect," following growing worldwide uncertainties regarding population, resources, and military/industrial activities. Heilbroner reexamines his judgments concerning the probable turn in the West toward more authoritarian political leadership. He is hopeful we may learn to live with "irreconcilable conflicts and contradictions"; he believes democracy's best hope may lie in acquiring "gifted" leadership that could motivate disparate groups to observe disciplines and ethical principles that would help us survive enormous social changes.

177. Heiss, Richard L. and McInnis, Noel F., eds. **Can Man Care for the Earth?** New York: Abingdon Press, 1976. 127 p.
A collection of vignettes, parables, and questions designed to show how adherence to the Judeo-Christian instructions in the Bible—obeying God's laws—will enable humans, as the lesser partner in the covenant with God, to live in harmony and to avoid ecological disaster.

178. Heller, Erich. **Goethe and the Idea of Scientific Truth.**
Swansea [Wales]: University College, [1949]. 36 p.
Inaugural and Bicentenary Lecture by the Head of the Department of German, delivered at the College on November 17, 1949. A scholarly discussion of Goethe's concern with scientific materialism. He, according to Heller, urged greater understanding of life and nature through experience and intuitive inner vision.

179. Henshaw, P. S. **This Side of Yesterday: Extinction or Utopia.** New York: Wiley, 1971. 186 p.
A systems approach to the study of the origins of human beings, their civilizations, and their place in nature. The message is clear that humanity has arrived at a point where major shifts in attitudes and conduct both in environmental and social concerns hold the only potential for survival and continuing human development. Index.

180. Hessel, Dieter T., ed. **Energy Ethics: A Christian Response.** New York: Friendship Press, 1979. 170 p.
A collection of papers resulting from a seminar convened by Hessel as part of the deliberations of the Energy Study Panel of the National Council of the Churches of Christ. His ideas are premised on the realization that energy-policy decisions will affect future human communities as well as our own. The discussions cover ethical, social, political, economic, and theological implications of policies that technologists alone cannot decide.

The book seeks to assist citizens generally and Christians in particular to become more cognizant of energy issues' dimensions.

181. Hine, Virginia and Gerlach, Luther P. **Many Concerned, Few Committed.** Natural History 79(10) December 1970: 16–17, 76–80.
Analysis of a questionnaire (published in the June–July issue 79(6), 27–29) which challenges a number of assumptions on values in our society. It reveals that 81 percent of the respondents disagreed with the statement that plants and animals exist primarily for human use and enjoyment. The researchers note a relation between environmental concerns and acceptance of social changes; in these concerns there is no generation gap. The responses to the questionnaire show that while few people are committed to action, their example is beginning to generate new attitudes and life styles.

182. Hollander, Jack M. **Scientists and the Environment: New Responsibilities.** Ambio 1(3) June 1972: 116–119.
This article suggests that research scientists involved in environmental problems should be more concerned with the social and ethical questions that many among them have ignored previously. They must be concerned with how their knowledge may be used and should work closely both with scholars in other disciplines and with the public to find solutions to these problems.

183. Hornblower, Margot. **The Beastly Harvest.** The Washington Post Magazine, July 8, 1979: 18–24.
In a dramatically illustrated article, Hornblower explores the illegal traffic in endangered species of both plants and animals and the cruelty in the legal trade of these species. She attributes the continuation of these practices to human indifference.

184. Houston Conference on Technology and Human Future, Houston, 1972. **To Create a Different Future: Religious Hope and Technological Planning.** Edited by Kenneth Vaux. New York: Friendship Press, 1972. 144 p.
A compendium of papers presented at the conference with a foreword by Margaret Mead. Three are especially pertinent. "Global Limitations and Human Responsibility," by Jorgen Randers discusses the problems that affect decision making. In "Technology and Conviviality," by Ivan Illich, the term "conviviality" is used to convey an attitude of openness and concern for life on this planet. "Religious Hope and Technological Planning," by Kenneth Vaux offers a spiritual vision and some ways humans can work for a more desirable future. Commentaries; footnotes at end of each chapter.

185. Hubbard, F. Patrick. **Justice, Limits to Growth and an Equilibrium State.** Philosophy and Public Affairs 7(4) Summer 1978: 326–345.

Hubbard recommends the concept of the "equilibrium state," first introduced by philosopher John Rawls ("A Theory of Justice," 1971) as a means of preventing the exhaustion of the earth's resources and doing justice to future generations. A "just savings principle" would require that each generation be responsible to the next by observing established limits to individual and social consumption. Hubbard also relates administrative strategies that might accomplish his goals with the least loss of political liberties. Notes.

186. Hughes, J. Donald. **Ecology in Ancient Civilization.** Albuquerque: University of New Mexico Press, 1975. 181 p.

This study aims to increase the understanding of early civilizations as antecedents of our current ecological crisis. Those most affecting Western culture—Greek, Roman, Jewish, and early Christian—are examined. The concluding chapter, particularly, discusses respect for the earth found in each of these philosophies and religions. Hughes suggests that a return to that respect may help meet today's needs. Notes; suggestions for further reading; index.

187. Hurst, J. S. **Towards a Theology of Conservation.** Theology 75(622) April 1972: 197–205.

Hurst chides the church for being nearly the last of the public opinion molders to face openly the full dimensions of environmental crisis. He cites biblical studies, poets, philosophers, and theologians to point up the difficulties of achieving consensus. His concern is the lack of public comprehension of humanity's ultimate responsibility toward itself and toward nature—curbing population and protecting the natural environment. Notes.

188. Huth, Hans. **Nature and the American: Three Centuries of Changing Attitudes.** Berkeley: University of California Press, 1957. 250 p.

A survey of the developments that led to political and social interest in conservation in the United States, particularly related to growth of the national park system, timberlands, and city parks. Includes a fine collection of plates showing nineteenth-century paintings, drawings, and photographs.

189. Huxley, Aldous L. **The Human Situation: Lectures at Santa Barbara.** Edited by Piero Ferrucci. New York: Harper, 1977. 261 p.

In "Man and his Planet" and "More Nature in Art," two of a series of lectures delivered in 1959, Huxley portrays the gloomy state of the planet, for which humans are responsible. He goes on to delineate the difficult necessities of facing these problems in metaphysical, ethical, and aesthetic ways.

190. Huygen, Wil. **Gnomes.** Illustrated by Rien Poortvliet. New York: Abrams, 1977. Unpaged.

By appearance this could be judged either a children's or a coffee-table book. It is a portrayal in words and pictures of love, kindness, and simple living—a moral on achieving balance and harmony with nature.

191. Ice, Jackson L. **The Ecological Crisis: Radical Monotheism vs. Ethical Pantheism.** Religion in Life 44(2) Summer 1975: 203–211.

A teacher of religion examines the history and roots of the ecological crisis in Western culture. Ice sees Judeo-Christian-humanistic ideals as confusing rather than enlightening. He cites Albert Schweitzer's observations on Western political and economic aggression and ethical superficiality. The article concludes with an elaboration of the Schweitzer ethic. Notes.

192. Illich, Ivan. **Tools for Conviviality.** New York: Harper, 1973. 110 p. (World Perspectives, v. 47. Edited by Ruth N. Anshen)

In the introduction the editor stresses that an intellectual and spiritual awakening is taking place in the world among people in science, philosophy, and related fields. This "crisis in consciousness" prompts reexamination of the "new" interdependent relationship between humans and the unique, fragile environment called Earth. In the following essay, Illich defines the limits to which industrial corporations and/or states can control and manipulate societies without the social system's and individual's succumbing to general anomie and disintegrative behavior. Essentially he is formulating a theory for living in the post-industrial age.

193. Iltis, Hugh H. **Shepherds Leading Sheep to Slaughter:** . . . American Biology Teacher 34(4) March 1972: 127–130, 137.

————. **The Extinction of Species and the Destruction of Ecosystems.** 34(5) April 1972: 201–205.

Two articles adapted from a keynote address at the National Association of Biology Teachers annual convention, Chicago, October 14, 1971. A strongly worded criticism of many government policies covering the natural environment. Also a plea to biology teachers to help reverse the processes of ecological destruction by teaching students the value of diversity in nature; the effects of decisions governed solely by political expediency; and how technology may be used to benefit the environment rather than to destroy it. References.

194. India. Ministry of Information and Broadcasting, Publications Division. **India's Wildlife.** Delhi: 1963. 62 p.

Chapter I, "Beneficial Role of Wildlife," and chapter II, "Wildlife and Environment," discuss the place of animals in India's religion, literature, art, and culture as well as in recreation, science, and economics. The rest of the book is devoted to descriptions of specific animals. Photographs.

195. The Institute of Environmental Education and The Association of New Jersey Environmental Commissions. **Tuning the Green Machine: An Integrated View of Environmental Systems.** Dobbs Ferry, N.Y.: Oceana Publications, 1978. 320 p.

A handbook designed to assist citizens in making informed and responsible environmental decisions. It also serves students as a survey of essential areas of environmental concern. These areas are delineated by chapters and sub-headings and include a glossary of terminology and information contributing to decision making at both the community and regional levels. Ethical considerations are suggested in "A Perspective," which prefaces each of fourteen chapters. Bibliographic sources; appendixes; index.

196. International Symposium on Man's Role in Changing the Face of the Earth, Princeton, N.J.: 1955. **Man's Role in Changing the Face of the Earth.** Edited by William L. Thomas with Carl O. Sauer, Marston Bates, and Lewis Mumford. Published for the Wenner-Gren Foundation for Anthropological Research and the National Science Foundation. Chicago: University of Chicago Press, 1970. 1193 p.

The background papers prepared by seventy eminent scholars treat various facets of the topic of the symposium: historical, economic, geographical, sociological, anthropological, cultural, ethical, and philosophical. References after each paper; illustrations; and an index.

197. Jackson, Barbara (Ward), *Lady.* **A New Creation? Reflections on the Environmental Issues.** Vatican City: Pontifical Commission, Justice and Peace, 1973. 71 p.

Fifth in a series of commentaries on the document "Justice in the World," 1971. Ward strongly suggests that post-Renaissance society will change greatly when economic and political systems confront issues of justice among the world's people. This involves unpredictable readjustments in the manner in which people treat each other as well as their natural environments. Christian vision is discussed as a historical and powerful influence on the abilities of the human race to put the social virtues in practice in the coming age.

198. ———. **Progress for a Small Planet.** Foreword by
Mostafa K. Tolba. New York: Norton, 1979. 305 p.
Opening with a historical summary of theories and realities of world economic, political, and social evolution, Ward appraises our current global problems in the context of developing an environmentally sound and economically viable basis for future growth and progress. She synthesizes and reexamines themes from her many studies of the urbanization process and the North-South conflict. This leads to a discussion of a "new economic order."

199. ——— and Dubos, René. **Only One Earth: The Care and Maintenance of a Small Planet.** Unofficial report
commissioned by the Secretary-General of the United
Nations Conference on the Human Environment. New
York: Norton, 1972. 225 p.
A committee of scientific and intellectual leaders from fifty-eight countries served as consultants in this project, and many submitted complete manuscripts. The authors drafted and revised the volume, to which they contributed their own writing. There are many references throughout to conservation, wilderness, and spiritual values, though these are not reflected in the index. The final chapter, "Strategies for Survival," is especially pertinent.

200. Jackson, Dixie S., ed. **Who Needs Nature?** New York:
Wiley, 1973. 234 p.
Fourth in a series presenting a collection of poetry, fiction, essays, and drama for college or high school courses in English composition. There are project suggestions and composition exercises based on themes of current environmental import. Essays include Aldo Leopold's "The Land Ethic," and contributions by Elizabeth B. Drew, Gaylord Nelson, John Foules, Berton Roueché, René Dubos, and others.

201. James, Bernard. **The Death of Progress.** New York:
Knopf, 1973. 166 p.
Discusses the idea of progress as a cultural strategy, the nature and evidence of the death-of-progress ideology, and the alternatives that face us as a consequence. James describes the changes inherent in the development of a steady-state system involving evolution, biology, and ecology. Bibliographical notes.

202. Jegen, Mary E. and Manno, Bruno, eds. **The Earth is the Lord's: Essays on Stewardship.** New York: Paulist Press, 1978. 215 p.

The essays in this collection grew from a 1976 seminar (sponsored by Bread for the World Educational Fund and the University of Dayton) on "Stewardship: a Christian Perspective on Ownership and Use of Essential Resources." The biblical, theological, and philosophical traditions of stewardship are challenged in the first section of the book. There follows a discussion on basic questions, especially hunger, political action, agriculture, and personal adjustments to the need for simple lifestyles. Notes and suggested readings.

203. Jensen, Franklin L. and Tilberg, Cedric W. **The Human Crisis in Ecology.** New York: Board of Social Ministry, Lutheran Church in America, 1972. 107 p.

An exposition of the environmental and social crisis, its causes, and resolution. Prepared to guide Lutheran churches in understanding the issues, to encourage members to pursue an ecologically sound way of life, to stimulate study and discussion, and to assist members and the church in dealing with government and industry. The study focuses on God, humans, and nature, viewed together with human freedom as the apex of God's creation. This freedom brings privileges and responsibility. The latter is outlined as ten imperatives of an ecologically-sound existence. Bibliography.

204. John Paul II, Pope. **The Redeemer of Man (Redemptor Hominis).** Catholic Standard, March 29, 1979. Entire issue.

The first encyclical of Pope John Paul II, given at Rome, March 4, 1979. In section II, part 8, the Pope discusses the instability of the political world and the poor state of the natural environment, particularly in areas of rapid industrialization. Section III, parts 15 and 16 expands on the themes of exploitation of natural resources and the need for an ethical approach to their uses by the currently powerful groups in society.

205. Johnson, Dick. **Lake Pedder: Why a National Park Must Be Saved.** Adelaide: Griffin Press, 1972. 96 p.

Several conservation organizations cooperated in the preparation and publication of this book. It is a plea to save a unique wilderness for aesthetic and scientific reasons. It also demonstrates the growing opposition in Australia to unregulated development and unrestricted economic growth. Bibliography.

206. Johnson, Josephine W. **The Inland Island.** Illustrated by Mel Klapholz. New York: Simon and Schuster, 1969. 159 p.

The personal view of the natural world by a writer who knows every mood and creature of her midwestern farm. She contemplates with dismay the role of humans versus nature in our society as she describes her land and all its life, the serene and the bitter, through a year's cycle.

207. Johnson, S. S. **Ethics and Ecology in the Conservation Movement in the United States of America.** Boston: 1970. 242 p.

Ph.D. dissertation at Boston University, 1970. Johnson traces environmental concerns to the Judeo-Christian concept of stewardship. He criticizes the organized church for neglecting this aspect of its basic beliefs. He hopes that in America, at least, the conservation movement is on the verge of finding an ethic based on the spiritual values of the natural world and that this ethic will eventually influence the control of human populations and government planning. Abstract in "Dissertation Abstracts International."

208. Johnson, Warren. **Muddling Toward Frugality.** San Francisco: Sierra Club, 1978. 252 p.

Johnson takes a long view of the state of our economy and is cautiously optimistic. The fading of the resource-abundant era does not mean the end of the world, for, with luck, a marketplace-enforced frugality should allow us the time we need to muddle toward political and cultural acceptance of labor-intensive technologies and reduced consumption of resources. His thesis encompasses vital areas of economics, social history, and ecology.

209. Jonas, Hans. **Technology and Responsibility: Reflections on the New Tasks of Ethics.** Social Research 40(1) Spring 1973: 31–54.

Paper presented to the International Congress of Learned Societies in the Field of Religion, Los Angeles, September 1–5, 1972. This philosopher contends that technology has changed the power of human action from one which had only immediate consequences to one which will determine the future. Consequently a new ethic must be found which will insure that there will be a future.

210. Kahn, Herman, Brown, William, and Martel, Leon. **The Next 200 Years: A Scenario for America and the World.** New York: Morrow, 1976. 241 p.

A report from the Hudson Institute offering the staff's perspective on a distant future of economic growth, technological development, and satisfactory management of nature for the benefit of all human beings. While there is some treatment of the aesthetic factors in environmental changes, the questions of morals or ethics are not considered. The book's proposals are basically anthropocentric.

211. Karff, Samuel E. **Man's Power and Limits in a Technological Age.** Judaism 23(2) Spring 1974: 161–173.

Karff's essay concentrates on three areas which humans have traditionally considered as God's decrees to them: 1) the "conditional" one of dominion over nature; 2) freedom; and 3) mortality. Each of these has been challenged in the technological age. This discussion, with many citations and examples, sets forth the modern reality of the struggle between what is moral and what is possible. In the first case, humans are accountable to God for their stewardship over the earthly world; secondly, human beings have the choice of becoming a noble race or the most dangerous creatures on earth; lastly, death illustrates our earthly attachment and signifies the human dependence on "God's infinite power and love." Notes.

212. Katzir-Katchalsky, Aharon. **An Israeli Scientist's Approach to Human Values.** Bulletin of the Atomic Scientists 28(8) October 1972: 19–23.

Adapted from an address given in Brussels in 1972. Katzir-Katchalsky analyzes the relation of science to culture in Israel particularly, and in other scientifically advanced countries. He examines global aspects of scientific technology and says that a new morality must accompany human recognition that all life exists in a fragile and closed system.

213. Kilpatrick, James J. **The Foxes' Union, and Other Stretchers. . .** McLean, Va.: EPM Publications, 1977. 174 p.

Partly humorous and partly philosophical discourses on country living in Scrabble, Va. A Washington, D. C.-based journalist, Kilpatrick discusses the things that matter, including love of place and the tie to the land that remain part of the essential elements in all of us, even city-dwellers.

214. Klostermaier, Klaus. **World Religions and the Ecological Crisis.** Religion 3(2) Autumn 1973: 132–145.

After a brief comparison of Eastern and Western concepts of behavior toward the environment, Klostermaier turns to study human attitudes regarding nature, first within primitive and ancient religions, then from industrial times to the present. He stresses the urgent need to change some aspects of our economic and cultural value systems. Notes.

215. Kohr, Leopold. **The Breakdown of Nations.** New York: Dutton, 1978. 250 p.

Reissue in paperback of the 1957 edition with the addition of an afterword. Kohr is one of the first academicians to question the West's predilection for large-scale politics, economics, and technology. He theorizes about many aspects of human uses of power. He considers Western expansion of "essential" consumer production and its paradoxical result: in many cases, living standards have fallen, not risen. He cites other inefficiencies resulting from "bigness" (this before E. F. Schumacher's "small is beautiful" argument). In the afterword, he reassesses his thesis as it pertains to human social, economic, and political conduct. Appendixes; bibliography; index.

216. Kormondy, Edward J. **Environmental Education: The Whole Man Revisited.** American Biology Teacher 33(1) January 1971: 15–17.
Adapted from an address to the National Association of Biology Teachers convention, Denver, October 21–24, 1970. A scientist and educator suggests that, since the churches have failed to do so, education must spread the new ethos of care for the universe and its inhabitants.

217. Krieger, Martin H. **What's Wrong With Plastic Trees?** Science 179 (4072) February 2, 1973: 446–455.
An urban planner thinks that there is no intrinsic value in nature; only certain segments of the population feel a need for the natural world; and social justice is the only criterion to be observed. Based on the utilitarian concept, we need to establish priorities for intervention in the natural environment, and in the end we may come to prefer artificial environments. References and notes.

218. Krutch, Joseph W. **The Best Nature Writing of Joseph Wood Krutch.** New York: Morrow, 1969. 384 p.
Essays on many aspects of the relationship between humans and nature. The introduction outlines the historical and theological confusion surrounding the theme that "man is the End of Creation," especially with regard to his feelings and behavior toward the rest of animal life. The final section contains essays on the "Meaning of Conservation" and concludes that "conservation is not enough." Illustrated.

219. ———. **Man's Ancient, Powerful Link to Nature—A Source of Fear and Joy.** *In* his If You Don't Mind my Saying so. . . New York: William Sloan, 1964. pp. 336–348.
An essay on one of the oldest love-hate relationships in the world and on the fateful tests to which it is being subjected today.

220. Kury, Channing. **Prolegomena to Conservation: A Fisheye Review.** Natural Resources Journal 17(3) July 1977: 493–509.
An examination of various applications of a definition: "Conservation philosophy is the examination of the assumptions and methodologies of

decision-making in regard to resources." Kury examines some conservation thinking of nineteenth- and twentieth-century America. He concludes that many ideas are inadequate by themselves to establish rational policies, but are aids to the development of such policies. Many reference notes.

221. Labine, Clem. **Preservationists are Un-American!**
Historic Preservation 31(1) March–April 1979: 18–20.
Contributing the "Guest Opinion," an "old house owner" declares that preservationists have already adopted the ethical values needed for survival of the planet: concern for the environment, repairing and recycling, not being afraid of physical work, and deriving a sense of well-being from other than material consumption.

222. Lacey, Michael J. **The Mysteries of Earth-Making Dissolve:** . . . Washington, D.C.: 1979. 451 p.
Ph.D. dissertation at George Washington University. Investigation into the ideas of a group responsible for the adoption of the utilitarian concept of conservation in the late nineteenth and early twentieth centuries. This group evolved into a close community which one member called "the national seminary of learning" and dominated the intellectual life of Washington, D.C., for many years. The ideas which surfaced and affected decision making culminated in Theodore Roosevelt's conservation program and, with a few exceptions such as the Forest Service, suffered the same fate as most of the Progressive Party program.

223. Lamm, Norman. **Man's Position in the Universe: A Comparative Study of the Views of Saadia Gaon and Maimonides.** The Jewish Quarterly Review 55(3) January 1965: 208–234.
According to this scholar, the earliest systematic delineation of anthropocentrism in Hebrew belief was that of Saadia. Lamm contrasts Saadian doctrine with that of Maimonides, which reflects Greek influence (especially the Aristotelian): that all of creation is in essence a part of God, that humans are part of that creation, and that they are distinguished from other creatures by intellect.

224. **Learning to Live With Less.** Futurist 11(4) August 1977: 200–230.
Five articles examining the possibilities for change in Western values and life styles in recognition of the inadequacies and injustices of our material civilization and in order to provide ecological, spiritual, and social rewards.

225. Leeds, Anthony and Vayda, Andrew P., eds. **Man, Culture, and Animals: The Role of Animals in Human Ecological Adjustments.** Washington, D.C.: American Association for the Advancement of Science, 1965. 304 p.

Book based on a symposium (of the same name) of the 128th AAAS annual meeting, Denver, Colorado, December 1961. Contains additional papers by anthropologists and geographers so that diverse cultures on the major continents of the world are represented.

226. Lehrs, Ernst. **Man or Matter:** . . . 2d ed., rev. and enl. New York: Harper, 1958. 456 p.

A historical inquiry into both learned and intuitive methods of acquiring scientific understanding based on Goethe's method of training observation and thought. A final section is entitled "Toward a New Cosmosophy."

227. Leliaert, Richard. **"All Things Are Yours. . ." Ecology: Catchword or Crisis?** The Homiletic and Pastoral Review 70(8) May 1970: 573–578, 597.

An essay on "biblical ecology" and a discussion of the human relationship to the natural world as expressed in both Old and New Testaments. The underlying questions of what are we and what are our responsibilities toward earth require both the scientific and religious communities to supply leadership and guidance to others for sound ecological actions.

. 228. Leiss, William. **The Domination of Nature.** New York: Braziller, 1972. 242 p.

This study elucidates some religious, historical, philosophical, and scientific roots of human attitudes toward nature. These mirror both the ideologies and contradictions in our behavior. The "conquest of nature" in the Baconian sense is not the answer to universal material satisfaction, particularly if the "wasteful consumption of advanced capitalist societies" is a standard. In the concluding chapter, "The Liberation of Nature?" Leiss develops the thought that human consciousness is a part of nature itself and that it must be guided to understand the destructiveness of many human activities.

229. Leopold, Aldo. **Round River: From the Journals of Aldo Leopold.** Edited by Luna B. Leopold. New York: Oxford University Press, 1953. 173 p.

Entries from Leopold's journals from his early years in the Forest Service and into his academic career show his philosophy evolving from conventional hunter and forester to pioneering thinker on conservation ethics.

230. ———. **A Sand County Almanac, With Essays on**   •
Conservation from Round River. New York: Sierra Club/
Ballantine, 1966. 295 p.

First published in 1949, "A Sand County Almanac" is a classic statement
on the need for drastic revisions in the ways we use the land. Among the
essays, see especially part IV which points to the failure of conservationists and others in the public and private sector to educate for a land
ethic that goes beyond economic motives.

231. Lewis, Clarence I. **Collected Papers.** Stanford, Calif.:
Stanford University Press, 1970. 444 p.

In "The Individual and the Social Order" especially, Lewis discusses his
Law of Objectivity which calls for compassion toward all creatures. No
subject index.

232. **Living with Nature.** Proceedings of the National
Summer School on Religion, 4th, Ursula College, 1973.
Edited by John Nurser. Canberra: Centre for Continuing
Education, Australian National University, 1973. 83 p.

Papers covering many aspects of the subject: the doomsday debate; Old
Testament views (with citations); the physical environment in Hindu literature; the Tao and the ecosystem; a Roman Catholic response; and
other pertinent investigations. Notes follow each essay.

233. Livingston, James C. **The Ecological Challenge to**
Christian Ethics. Christian Century 88(48) December 1, 1971: •
1409–1412.

Suggests that Christian thinkers need to understand ecological laws or
axioms in order to survive and to restore to humans the basic goodness
and valuable interrelationships of the natural world.

234. Livingston, John A. **One Cosmic Instant: Man's Fleeting**
Supremacy. Boston: Houghton, 1973. 243 p.

An ecologist views the changing states of life on earth and finds the sources
of destruction of the natural world in human attitudes traceable from
geologic time. Livingston believes that we must educate ourselves to
sustain, not mutilate, the fragile balances of life's processes. Index.

235. Lowenthal, David. **Is Wilderness "Paradise Enow"?**
Images of Nature in America. Columbia University Forum
7(2) Spring 1964: 34–40.

According to this author, human treatment of nature must be anthropocentric and must conform only to human values; there is no intrinsic merit
in grass, trees, flowing water, etc.

236. Lundborg, Louis B. **Future Without Shock.** New York: Norton, 1974. 155 p.

A banker writes of his own "greening"; of the rights to private ownership of property; of the concept of stewardship of land, space, and other resources; and of some of the ethical obligations that "big business" and the powerful everywhere must assume. Index.

237. Lutz, Paul and Santmire, H. Paul. **Ecological Renewal.** Philadelphia: Fortress Press, 1972. 153 p.

Both authors apply the "Spaceship Earth" imagery to develop scientific and religious dimensions of the ecological crisis. Lutz, a biologist, in "An Interdependent World" stresses the interrelatedness of all life forms and places human beings at the center of the ecological crisis. He urges application of the "collective insights of theology, philosophy and ethics" to meet challenges of human ecology and suggests that the church should take a leadership role. In "Catastrophe and Ecstasy," Santmire, a theologian, advocates a reorientation in human values if we are to survive the ecological crisis with justice and freedom. This requires stabilization and reduction of population growth; a drastic cutback in non-essentials of economic growth; the substitution of cooperation for competition as an ethical guideline; a redistribution of wealth; and, above all, the acceptance of a universal good and universal love. See also comments by the editor of Fortress Press.

238. MacBryde, Bruce. **Plants for All Seasons: Conservation as if Nature Mattered.** The Nature Conservancy News 29(2) March/April 1979: 9–11.

A botanist discusses plants in relation to the Endangered Species Act of 1973. He expounds the philosophy that, like animals, plants have a right to exist.

239. McCormick, Richard A. **Notes on Moral Theology.** Theological Studies 32(1) 1971: 97–107.

A summary of facts behind environmental deterioration in America, followed by brief references to some major voices calling for "an ethics of ecology." These include Lynn White on "orthodox Christian arrogance," and synopses of views by Frederick Elder, Bruce Wrightsman, and others. Proposed solutions by other authorities are also outlined.

240. McHarg, Ian L. **Design With Nature.** Garden City, N.Y.: Natural History Press, 1969. 197 p.

An investigation in words and pictures by a landscape architect and planner. He is concerned with the ecological planning of landscape and the varied possibilities of coordinating human physical and aesthetic needs with ecological principles. Lewis Mumford's introduction characterizes the book as making a unique contribution through the "mixture of scientific insight and constructive environmental design."

241. ———. **Man: Planetary Disease.** Washington, D.C.:
Agricultural Research Service, U. S. Dept. of Agriculture,
1971. 28 p.

The 1971 B. Y. Morrison Memorial Lecture presented in cooperation with the Wildlife Management Institute at the North American Wildlife and Natural Resources Conference, Portland, Oregon, March 10, 1971. A critical survey of Western views of humans and nature. McHarg is pessimistic that sufficient numbers of people will learn enough and care enough to survive in creative harmony within the natural biosphere. The lecture is a challenge to humanity to wake up before it is too late.

242. McHenry, Robert and Van Doren, Charles, eds. **A Documentary History of Conservation in America.** New York: Praeger, 1972. 422 p.

A broad selection from articles, poems, essays, and newspapers covering several centuries and several English-speaking countries. See especially "The Land Ethic," in part three for statements that include authors William O. Douglas, Paul R. Ehrlich, Aldo Leopold, Thomas Merton, and Paul Lambert.

243. McKenna, Harold J. **Yesterday—Extinction, Today—Extermination, Tomorrow—What?** Journal of Environmental Education 7(3) Spring 1976: 28–33.

A professor of environmental studies differentiates between extinction, a natural phenomenon, and extermination, a power assumed by the human race. Only by developing new values and controlling our technologies and populations can we avoid this role.

244. McKenzie, John L. **God and Nature in the Old Testament.** Catholic Biblical Quarterly 14(1) January 1952: 18–39, and 14(2) April: 124–145.

Analysis of beliefs of early Hebrews and other ancient peoples who lived close to nature and yet developed the idea of a single deity—a creator—who related to human beings and to their history. The Hebrews alone, however, viewed this deity as absolute, independent, and a unity. In the Old Testament, nature expresses the Hebrew concept of wisdom in that, amid great diversity, she exhibits a visable order and regularity beyond human understanding. Yahweh dominates nature; when angered by human immorality, Yahweh may manifest his passion through natural phenomena. These ideas changed over time, but always there were strong links of interaction among God, humans, and nature—until relatively modern times when the "ambitions" of science and technology boasted of the "conquest of nature."

245. McLuhan, T. C., comp. **Touch the Earth: A Self-Portrait of Indian Existence.** New York: Outerbridge & Dienstfrey; distributed by E. P. Dutton, 1971. 185 p.
Collection of speeches, writings, and pictures illustrating the American Indians' life, their respect for the land and its inhabitants, and their relationships with each other.

246. McPhee, John. **Encounters with the Archdruid.** New York: Farrar, 1971. 245 p.
In three sections, "A Mountain," "An Island," and "A River," the conservation view as expounded by David Brower is pitted against that of a mining engineer, a resort developer, and a dam builder. Their conversations, observations, and attitudes toward wilderness, natural resources, human societies, flora and fauna, are related, and together reveal most of the major issues facing environmental planning. The varied localities, two in the western United States and one in the Southeast, add specific color and meaning.
The paperback edition has the subtitle: "Narratives About a Conservationist and his Natural Enemies."

247. Maddox, John R. **The Doomsday Syndrome.** New York: McGraw-Hill, 1972. 292 p.
Maddox recognizes the seriousness of the state of the environment, but considers calamitous prophesies of environmental "extremists" overstated, at times contradictory, or not grounded on fact. Some of his targets are Barry Commoner, Paul Ehrlich, and Rachel Carson. The most serious concern about the doomsday syndrome, he concludes, is that it will "undermine our spirit." As he says in the preface, "This is not a scholarly work but a complaint."

248. **Man and His Environment.** Dialog 9(3) Summer 1970: 163–239.
An entire issue on the theme, with essays by Douglas Daetz, H. Paul Santmire, Daniel F. Martensen, Bruce Wrightsman, Ronal S. Laura, and Thomas E. Nutt. Together they provide an overview of the major issues and their points of debate. The final article, "Starting Points for an Ecological Theology," is a bibliographic survey of current literature.

249. **Man and Nature: Metaphysical Ecology.** *In* Philosophy for a New Generation. 2d ed. Edited by Arthur K. Bierman and James A. Gould. New York: Macmillan, 1973. pp. 547–606.
Part of a collection of essays for a college text on philosophy. Various

philosophers expound their interpretations of nature and of humanity in nature. The editors comment: "After reading. . .these two sections, you will see that ecological togetherness continually faces the threat of metaphysical divorce." See also the essays in the next section, "Philosophy and Theological Thought."

250. **Man in His Environment.** Social Action 34(9) May 1958: 3–46.

The entire issue is devoted to showing how self-interest, ethics, and aesthetics demand a change in political actions toward the natural environment. Particularly pertinent is the article by Robert Anderson, a Congregational minister, entitled "An Ecological Conscience for America," in which he suggests ways the church can stimulate thought and action.

251. **Man, Society and the Environment:** . . . Moscow: Progress Publishers, 1975. 340 p.

Papers collected by researchers from the Institute of Geography of the USSR Academy of Sciences. They are based on the Marxist interpretation of the interaction between society and nature. Part one covers primitive and capitalist societies' attitude toward nature. Part two deals with Soviet experience in exploration and development of natural resources and improvement of the environment. Part three describes practical and cultural aspects and includes establishing wildlife preserves and problems related to international seas. Part four is devoted to socio-economic aspects. Bibliography at the end of each paper.

252. Mann, David. **Ethical and Social Responsibility in the Planning and Design of Engineering Projects.** Engineering Issues 98(PP1) January 1972: 33–41.

An engineering student suggests that concern for environmental protection be added to the Code of Practice of the American Society of Civil Engineers' ethical guidelines, which already include an obligation for community service. References.

253. Mariner, James L. **Capitalism, Science-Teaching and the Environment.** American Biology Teacher 33(9) December 1971: 555–556.

A science teacher posits that science should be taught as a discipline which relates also to the humanities. Students should be helped to recognize that science alone cannot solve environmental and other crises. Teach facts, but relate them to larger areas of adult responsibilities in economics, history, and human rights.

254. Marx and Engels on Ecology. Edited and compiled by
Howard L. Parsons. Westport, Conn.: Greenwood Press,
1977. 262 p.

Part 1 (Introduction): analysis of the ecological concerns of Marx and
Engels. The editor believes their applicability to contemporary problems
points to a transition from capitalist destruction of both nature and humanity to communist care for both. Notes. Part 2: selections from Marx'
and Engels' writings on ecology. Part 3: bibliography—a list of recent
ecological literature, including ethics.

**255. Marx, Leo. The Machine in the Garden: Technology and
the Pastoral Ideal in America.** New York: Oxford University
Press, 1964. 392 p.

Around the fresh, virgin continent, Europeans wove their myths, fantasies,
and ideals and girded themselves for the challenge to create a new culture.
Marx examines "the uses of the pastoral ideal in the interpretation of the
American experience." He deals with both the popular-sentimental and
the imaginative-complex kinds of pastoralism, using selected examples
of literary figures and their works. Extensive notes and index.

256. Matthiessen, Peter. Wildlife in America. Introduction by
Richard H. Pough. Drawings by Bob Hines. New York:
Viking, 1959. 304 p.

A chronicle of the effect of human activities on North American wildlife
from the arrival of the first Europeans to the present; it follows the tide
of settlement from the Eastern seaboard, across the interior, to the Pacific.
Described are the actions and impact of the fur trappers, market hunters,
whalers, and developers on many creatures. Public attitudes to these
activities are traced as well. How many animals vanished and what was
being done by the late 1950s to protect wildlife conclude the tale. Reference
notes; extensive bibliography; index.

**257. Mead, Margaret. Twentieth Century Faith: Hope and
Survival.** New York: Harper, 1972. 172 p. (Religious
Perspectives, v. 25)

Preface by Ruth N. Anshen, who planned and edited the series. Most of
the book is concerned with human relationships, but especially in two
chapters, "Christians in a Technological Era," and "Promise," the author
discusses the role of humans in the natural world.

**258. Meadows, Dennis L. and Meadows, Donella H. Toward
Global Equilibrium.** Cambridge, Mass.: Wright-Allen Press,
1973. 358 p.

Papers by members of the System Dynamics Group in the Alfred P. Sloan

68

School of Management at the Massachusetts Institute of Technology. This volume details and enlarges upon some aspects of the "world modeling project" as described in a previous work, "The Limits to Growth," 1972. Subject areas include: pollution by chemical contaminants; population growth and control; solid wastes; and finite resources. See especially the final two chapters: "The Carrying Capacity of the Global Environment: a Look at Ethical Alternatives" and "Churches at the Transition Between Growth and World Equilibrium." Figures and graphs.

259. Means, Richard L. **The Ethical Imperative: The Crisis in American Values.** Garden City, N.Y.: Doubleday, 1969. 277 p.

A sociological study with notes following each chapter. In chapter 5, "Man and Nature," Means discusses "how culture shapes our sense of the control of nature" and other factors of modern life that make it difficult for many to relate to the natural world and to other living creatures. Index.

260. Merton, Thomas, **The Wild Places.** . . Center Magazine 1(5) July 1968: 40–44.

A member of a Trappist community discusses the inherent conflicts in Americans' attitudes toward nature: we continue to honor the wilderness legend while we destroy the nature around us. He points to the existence of these conflicts in the Bible, in Puritan thought, and among the pioneers and today's capitalists—and even among conservationists themselves.

261. Michael, Donald N. **On Growth and the Limits of Organizational Responsiveness.** Technological Forecasting and Social Change 10(1) 1977: 1–14.

Paper originally presented at "Limits to Growth '75," the first biennial assessment of alternatives to growth, The Woodlands, Texas, October 19–20, 1975. Michael's thesis is that a new set of beliefs and values which emphasize steady-state philosophy would contribute to more effective organizational behavior. He speculates that in consequence of accepting the knowledge of interdependence and of the finiteness of resources, humans can free themselves from the bondage of their possessions and of the restrictive belief in unlimited material growth.

262. Miles, John C. **Humanism and Environmental Education.** Journal of Environmental Education 7(3) Spring 1976: 2–10.

An educator looks at the state of environmental education in the United States. He concludes that this study must combine with humanistic philosophies to prepare society for the coming decades of change. References.

263. Milne, Lorus J. and Milne, Margery. **Will the Environment Defeat Mankind?** Harvard Magazine 181(3) January–February 1979: 19–23.

These biologists emphasize that food and all forms of life depend on photosynthesis. Their explanation of the interrelationship of natural systems and the effects of human impact on them lead to the conclusion that conservation alone is "not enough." Our complex civilization needs an ethic both based on scientific understanding and not in conflict with religious views. Albert Schweitzer's "reverence for life" credo is their choice.

264. Mishan, E. J. **The Economic Growth Debate: An Assessment.** London: George Allen & Unwin, 1977. 277 p.

An economist challenges professionals and laymen alike who hold that economic growth as understood in the West is always a good thing. More is not necessarily better; society is paying a big price in terms of a "growing sense of malaise and unfulfillment," despite increasing social welfare and consumer freedom. Part 2, chapter 37, "Economic Growth and the Good Life: Fundamental Disharmonies—the Great Myths," contains the thought that for too long societies have neglected the values of divine law which stimulate "consensus on the fundamentals of moral law." See economic growth, environment, pollution in the index. References.

265. Mitchell, John G. **Bitter Harvest: Hunting in America.** Audubon 81(3) May 1979, 50–83; (4) July: 64–81; (5) September: 88–105; (6) November: 104–129; 82(1) January 1980: 80–97.

A series which analyzes why people hunt—and how hunters relate to other people's attitudes, to habitat destruction, and similar topics. Also discussed are people and organizations opposed to hunting: their rationale and activities. Both sides claim to have ethical reasons for what they are doing. The November issue is devoted to Native Americans, their modern hunting practices, and their relevance to a subsistence life style.

266. Momaday, N. Scott. **Native American Attitudes to the Environment.** *In* Seeing with a Native Eye. Edited by Walter H. Capps. New York: Harper, 1976. pp. 79–85.

Brief summary, adapted from discussions with students, of Indian beliefs in the interdependence of the world and its inhabitants and consequent respect for and obedience to the laws of nature. Several other essays and the introduction touch on these beliefs also. Scott Momaday's poetry, of which there are several volumes, should also be consulted.

267. Momaday, Natachee S. **American Indian Authors.** Boston: Houghton, 1972. 151 p.

This collection of short stories, legends, essays, poetry, and excerpts from longer pieces is an introduction to the literature of many groups. At the end of each entry is a brief biographical sketch of each author and a few discussion questions suitable for class work. For ethics see especially Chief Joseph, Thomas Whitecloud, Juanita Platero, Siyowin Miller, and N. Scott Momaday.

268. Montefiore, Hugh, ed. **Man and Nature.** London: Collins, 1975. 213 p.

A report (by the Anglican Man and Nature Working Group) outlining a Christian perspective on the problems of people in their environment begins this volume. The chapter "From Theology to Ethics" includes some insights from non-Christian cultures and the observation that contemporary "Western society has scarcely any common belief remaining about the origin, nature and destiny of man." The work ends with nine essays on various aspects of man and nature by Group members and others.

269. ———. **The Question Mark: The End of Homo Sapiens.** London: Collins, 1969. 104 p.

The Theological Lectures 1969, delivered under the auspices of the Church of Ireland in Queen's University, Belfast. The three lectures address the major problems of the next half century as they bear on the future existence of humanity. These include: the disparity of living standards in the world; tremendous waste of resources in the capitalist west; population problems; war dangers; peoples' regard for the environment and their ability to learn restraint; and finally, the theological aspects. Notes and index.

270. Moore, Ruth E. **Man in the Environment.** New York: Knopf, 1975. 155 p.

With the cooperation of the Field Museum. The first several chapters trace the origin and natural history of the earth, emphasizing its complicated and self-dependent interrelated biosphere. Succeeding chapters delineate historically the effect of humans on the environment and on each other. Finally, in "Imperatives and Alternatives" and "Implications of Change," Moore describes a new ethic based on the idea of brotherhood common to most great religions and extends this concept to encompass all living things.

271. **Mother Earth News.** v. 1, n. 1+ January 1970+ North Madison, Ohio. Bi-monthly.

Short articles, news items and humor are focused principally on alternative life styles, innovative technologies, ecology, economics, and on "working with nature and doing more with less."

272. Mountfort, Guy. **The Vanishing Jungle: The Story of the World Wildlife Fund Expeditions to Pakistan.** Boston: Houghton, 1970. 286 p.

Mountfort opens with a brief history of the Cholistan region's slow transition from a once fairly fertile region to one of largely desert conditions. The book aims to awaken the world's people to a critical situation in which vast sums preserve man made treasures in museums and places of historical interest while a relatively minute amount is devoted to the live, irreplaceable treasures, many of which are losing their habitat or are being hunted to extinction for luxury markets. The human population problem is recognized as the most pervasive one of all. Color and black and white photographs; notes on photography by Eric Hosking; appendixes; bibliography; index.

273. Muelder, Walter G. **Religion and Economic Responsibility.** New York: Scribner, 1958. 264 p.

Essays delivered at King's Chapel in Boston under the sponsorship of the Lowell Institute in 1951. While calling for moral and religious objectivity, they reflect the ethical dilemma of the times. Muelder's objective is to stimulate the application of ethics to the development of a responsible social order. Suggested readings and index.

274. Mumford, Lewis. **The Myth of the Machine: Technics and Human Development.** London: Secker & Warburg, 1967. 342 p.

Mumford questions modern man's distorted picture of himself as a conqueror of nature, a transformer, and a manipulator. This work pursues the "disciplined speculation" that man the ritual- and language-maker and socially organizing creature preceded man the tool-maker. He offers evidence that the human mind first expressed itself in domestic and artistic symbols rather than in the fashioning of utilitarian objects. Bibliography and index.

275. Myers, Norman. **The Long African Day.** New York: Macmillan, 1972. 404 p.

An account of the state of animal life in Africa from pre-history to the present; it is illustrated with photographs by the author. Myers warns that this magnificent scene may be at the twilight of its existence and should the long night follow we will all be the losers. He examines wildlife sanctuaries, not as isolated "outdoor zoos," but as integrated with people's lives. He observes that our descendents will hold us responsible for preservation of their heritage. Bibliography and index.

276. Nash, Roderick. **Do Rocks Have Rights?** Center Magazine 10(6) November–December 1977: 2–12.

Nash outlines the intellectual roots of environmental ethics in the West.

He cites a few key figures in a brief history of the growth of ethical ideas that question the prevailing anthropocentrism and environmental exploitation. He then elaborates on the theme of ethical evolution, beginning with early rules of behavior toward self, family, and tribe, and ending in a future time when the whole environment—the inanimate as well as the animate—will have rights of existence as humans learn to limit their freedoms. Aldo Leopold is especially credited for stimulating a dialogue among many interests from which environmental ethics may emerge as essential to humanity.

277. ———. **Wilderness and the American Mind.** New
Haven: Yale University Press, 1967. 256 p.
Nash traces the evolution of wilderness concepts from the first Puritan settlers, to Thoreau and Muir, to modern ecologists and conservationists, and to their opponents in "big" business and politics.

278. Nasr, Seyyed H. **Man and Nature: The Spiritual Crisis of Modern Man.** London: A Mandala Book published by
Unwin Paperbacks, 1976. 151 p.
Modern people would rather ignore environmental restrictions than face changes in their ways of living. Here is a major problem responsible, in large part, for the environmental crisis of today. The book—by the head of the philosophy department at Teheran University—is based on four lectures delivered at the University of Chicago, May 1966. Scientific and philosophic contributions by Islamic thinkers are cited. "In Islam the inseparable link between man and nature, and also between the sciences of nature and religion, is to be found in the Quran itself. . . ." Nasr refers to similar themes in other religions. He does not agree with the thinking of those (Teilhard de Chardin, for example) who, he says, present "pseudo-philosophies" which attempt to arrive at a synthesis of science and religion, the "antithesis of the spiritual vision of nature. . . ." Notes follow each chapter; index.

279. The National Council of the Churches of Christ. **Energy and Ethics: The Ethical Implications of Energy Production and Use.** New York: The Council, 1979. 48 p.
A concise presentation on energy problems, emphasizing the role of the Christian church. While the authors admit that the church was partially responsible for errors of the past through the "corruption of dominion into domination," they find that if Christians live by the laws of right relationships among all (including those yet unborn), they will be living by Christian principles. The booklet may be used as a study guide: it has questions at the end of each chapter. Footnotes; bibliography; selected resources list.
   Available from NCCC Energy Project, 475 Riverside Drive, New York, N.Y. 10027.

280. ——. Governing Board. **The Ethical Implications of Energy Production and Use.** New York: The Council, 1979. 9 p.

Policy statement adopted May 11, 1979. Its purpose is to clarify values and set forth guidelines for decision making, to indicate criteria by which energy technologies can be assessed, and to assist churches and individuals in reaching opinions and undertaking actions regarding energy production and use. It suggests that decisions must be based on ecological justice and grounded in Christian beliefs.

Available from NCCC Energy Project, 475 Riverside Drive, New York, N.Y. 10027.

281. The Nature Conservancy. **The Preservation of Natural Diversity: A Survey and Recommendations.** Final report prepared for U. S. Dept. of the Interior, 1975. Various pagings.

The introduction and part I deal with the reasons for maintaining ecological diversity as a national imperative. The authors propound that while there are powerful scientific reasons for preserving heterogeneity, these probably have their origin in the fact that the human aesthetic sense and instinct for survival are inextricably bound. Part II covers recommendations for implementing the findings.

282. Nelson, Leonard. **System of Ethics.** Translated by Norbert Guterman [from the German] with a foreword by A. J. Paton and introduction by Julius Kraft. New Haven: Yale University Press, 1956. 285 p.

A young German philosopher offers a summary of ethical principles and their application. His system of formal ethics encompasses the whole of human conduct. He specifically treats attitudes toward nature and the rights of animals. Subjects can easily be identified in the index.

283. Neuhaus, Richard J. **In Defense of People: Ecology and the Seduction of Radicalism.** New York: Macmillan, 1971. 315 p.

Neuhaus writes of the dichotomies in American culture and in our system of values. Political and social turbulence of the 1960s, the moral dilemmas of the Vietnam war, and the reality of poverty in America have prompted this cautionary polemic directed toward people who, in Neuhaus' opinion, speak as if crusades for "environmental quality" should circumvent democratic concerns for social justice in the world.

284. ——. **Resources and Global Development.** *In* his Christian Faith and Public Policy. . . Minneapolis: Augsburg, 1977. pp. 92–101.

The editor of Worldview magazine selects contemporary issues of concern. He declares that the divine mandate is for care and stewardship of the environment. He advocates that churches work for greater honesty and clarity in public policy making, both in environmental issues and in the redistribution of income and control of waste.

285. Nicholson, Max. **The Environmental Revolution: A Guide for the New Masters of the World.** London: Hodder and Stoughton, 1970. 366 p.

Nicholson is impressed by the dynamism of the environmental revolution which, he feels, was long delayed by organized religions, educational systems, political parties, and other institutions. The ecological problem is no longer simply one of nature threatened by humans; in many environments, all living things are endangered by technological elements which often seem uncontrollable. An immediate priority is to recast educational training and organizations to restore human control over technology. Nicholson recommends several other courses of action. Annexes; notes; charts; maps; photographs; index.

286. Odum, Eugene P. **Ecology: The Link Between the Natural and the Social Sciences.** New York: Holt, 1975. 244 p.

An enlarged version of the 1963 edition continuing the theme that humans are part of rather than apart from the natural environment. Ecology has become recognized as an integrative discipline, linking physical, biological, and social sciences. Suggested readings after each chapter; graphs; illustrations; appendixes; index.

287. ———. **The Emergence of Ecology as a New Integrative Discipline.** Science 195 (4280) March 25, 1977: 1289–1293.

Odum continues to call for a holistic approach to the study of ecosystems. He criticizes scientists for being too specialized and ignorant of philosophy.

288. Odum, Howard T. **Environment, Power, and Society.** New York: Wiley, 1971. 331 p.

Odum, a professor of environmental engineering, develops the concept of reducing natural systems and human institutions to energy budgets, an approach subject to factual ecological analysis. Will the output of a factory contribute an energy gain or loss to our whole ecosystem compared with the output from the farm or marsh lands it supplanted? The money factor often takes on a new perspective when we consider the complete balance sheet. The cumulative effects of our treatment of our natural surroundings and the stability of the planetary network can be very expensive, especially when comparing monetary benefits with costs in terms of energy loss. See his "Ten Commandments of the Energy Ethic for Survival of Man in Nature." Diagrams; references; index.

289. Olson, Sigurd F. **Sigurd F. Olson's Wilderness Days.**
New York: Knopf, 1972. 233 p.
Narrative by a naturalist and student of the silent lands that lie to the
north and northwest of Lake Superior, especially the lake region of Que-
tico-Superior. Here one travels by pack and canoe. Olson describes his
impressions and the natural events of the four seasons there and illustrates
these with sketches and color photographs. His central theme is based
on Thoreau's statement: "In wildness is the preservation of the world."

290. **On the Fifth Day: Animal Rights and Human Ethics.**
Edited by Richard K. Morris and Michael W. Fox.
Washington, D.C.: Acropolis Books, 1978. 240 p.
A collection of essays reflecting thinking in religion, science, and philos-
ophy on the interrelatedness of all life. See especially the final essay,
"What Future for Man and Earth?" in which Fox defines a human im-
perative to be a sense of global community and ecological awareness.
Biographical notes on contributors; index.

291. Ophuls, William. **Ecology and the Politics of Scarcity:
Prologue to a Political Theory of the Steady State.** San
Francisco: Freeman, 1977. 303 p.
A critique of American political values and institutions, which may be ill-
adapted to the situation of scarcity now confronting us. He offers no
practical solutions, but the last chapter, "Toward a Politics of the Steady
State," indicates the kind of new thinking and ideals that will make the
transition possible. Ophuls' critical analyses of the sources he used appear
as notes at the end of each chapter. Bibliography and index.

292. ———. **The Scarcity Society.** Harper's 245 (1487) April
1974: 47–52.
After a brief report on how scarcity may require unpalatable political
measures that would destroy liberty, Ophuls suggests another solution—
restoration of the virtues implicit in Buddhism, American Indian philosophy, and Christianity.

293. Osborn, Fairfield. **Our Plundered Planet.** London:
Faber, 1948. 192 p.
An early warning pointing to the growing unhealthy conditions in the
world's natural environments. This work surveys the evolution of dis-
harmony between human needs and the processes of nature in parts of
Asia, the Mediterranean, Africa, Russia, Europe, and the "New World."
It calls people and nations to wake up to the ultimate disaster inherent
in continued "defiance" of nature. Bibliography.

294. Owens, Owen D. **Stones into Bread? What Does the Bible Say About Feeding the Hungry Today?** Valley Forge, Pa.: Judson Press, 1977. 124 p.

Despite its title, this guide is not restricted to the problem of world hunger. Owens, a theologian, treats depletion of all natural resources as well as shortages of food. He reexamines the Bible for guidance and urges lay people to do the same. Each chapter is synthesized by a series of questions at the end. Useful for teachers.

295. **Papers from the Institute of Religion in an Age of Science,** Conference on the Ecosystem, Energy and Human Values. Zygon 12(2) June 1977: 106–179.

Contents: Karl E. Perters, professor of religion, "The Need for a Systems Approach: an Introduction. . ." and "Realities and Ideals in the World System." Howard T. Odum, professor of engineering sciences, "The Ecosystem, Energy, and Human Values." Thomas D. Harblin, "Mine or Garden? Values and the Environment—Probable Sources of Change in the Next Hundred Years." Don E. Marietta, professor of philosophy, "Religion Models and Ecological Decision Making." Philip N. Joranson, "The Faith-Man-Nature Group and a Religious Environmental Ethic." Notes follow all articles.

296. **Papers from the Meeting of the Science and Religion Forum on Man's Responsibility for Nature.** Zygon 12(3) September 1977: 182–258.

Contents: "Impact of Science and Technology on Society: New Directions in Ecumenical Social Ethics" by Paul Abrecht of the World Council of Churches. "Man and Nature: a Theological Assessment" by Hugh Montefiore, Bishop of Kingston. "Ecology, Theology, and Humanism" by D. Bryce-Smith, professor of organic chemistry. Also an article by Edward Goldsmith, editor of the Ecologist, "The Religion of a Stable Society." Notes follow all entries.

297. **Papers of the 1970 Conference on Ethics and Ecology of the Institute on Religion in an Age of Science.** Zygon 5(4) December 1970: 274–375.

A collection of six critical and searching papers on environmental crises covering diverse themes, both ecological and theological. Writers are: Joseph L. Fisher, Jack B. Bresler, Karl H. Hertz, William E. Martin, Wallace W. Robbins, and Daniel F. Martensen. Notes.

298. Parker, Charles F. **Come Unto Me: A Book for Personal Devotions.** New York: Rinehart, 1949. 104 p.

Attractive photographs from thirty areas in the U. S. national park system.

The pastor-author has selected a brief text, a poem, a prayer, and a biblical quotation related to the theme of each photo for the page opposite each photograph.

299. Parks, Marion. **Summary [of the Report of the Holy See for the United Nations Conference on the Human Environment, Stockholm, 1972].** *In* The Human Environment, v. II. Washington, D.C.: Woodrow Wilson International Center for Scholars, 1972. pp. 32–34.

Because of its mission, the Holy See addressed itself to the philosophical and ethical implications of environmental problems. It asserted that the nations assembled have an obligation to create an organization that will conserve God's gifts of the natural world and the cultural treasures resulting from human activity. All must work for more equitable distribution of property and provide for future generations. Many nations submitted reports, but this is the only one known to deal with the moral issues.

300. Parsons, Howard L. **Man East and West: Essays in East-West Philosophy.** Amsterdam: Grüner, 1975. 211 p.

Volume 8 in a series called Philosophical Currents. It is a study of human complexities—logic and language—in both the historical and the reflective sense. The core analyses are of various differences between some Eastern and Western societies in reference to nature, values, and human fulfillment. Parsons' discussions include: "The Natural and Human Roots of Popular Religions"; "The Unity of Man and Nature in East and West"; and "Man, Nature, Value and Religion." Index.

301. Passmore, John. **Man's Responsibility for Nature: Ecological Problems and Western Traditions.** New York: Scribner, 1974. 213 p.

A philosopher describes his concern for the future of the biosphere; he is alarmed that many of the suggested solutions to our problems seem to repudiate all that Western thought has produced and taught. Part one is a historical delineation of the various and sometimes conflicting Western attitudes toward nature. Part two is devoted to four particular problems— "Pollution, Conservation, Preservation, Multiplication." Part three, "The Traditions Reconsidered: Removing the Rubbish," considers the moral, philosophical, and political actions involved in solving problems raised in part two.

302. Patey, Edward H. **Christian Life-Style.** London: Mowbrays, 1976. 125 p.

The Dean of Liverpool offers a guide for group and/or individual study in answer to a series of questions. The first of these is "What Should be the Christian's Attitude Toward the Creation?'' Notes and discussions at the end of each chapter.

303. The Philosophy of C. I. Lewis. Edited by Paul A.
Schlipp. La Salle, Ill.: Open Court, 1968. 709 p.

A collection of descriptive and critical essays on the work of C. I. Lewis with a short rejoinder by the philosopher himself. References to ethics, to nature, to humans, and their values are scattered throughout and may be reached through the detailed subject index. Bibliography of C. I. Lewis' works.

304. Pirages, Dennis C. and Ehrlich, Paul R. **Ark II: Social Response to Environmental Imperatives.** New York: Viking, 1974. 344 p.

Just as Noah had ample warning to build his ark and save himself and animal species from the flood, so should we heed the indications that our exploitive actions are rapidly pushing us into an irrevocable ecological crisis. The social, economic, political, and attitudinal changes required to reverse this trend is what *Ark II* is all about. Explanatory notes; suggested reading list; index.

305. Platt, John. **World Transformation: Changes in Belief Systems.** Futurist 8(3) June 1974: 124–125.

An American Association for the Advancement of Science annual meeting address given February 27, 1974 by a staff member of the Mental Health Research Institute. Platt defines ecological ethics as recognition of the need to protect ''the seamless web of nature.'' This belief, in his opinion, is basic to a society founded on philosophical and religious principles.

306. Pollock, Norman C. **Animals, Environment and Man in Africa.** Farnborough, England: Saxon House, 1974. 159 p.

An analysis of the many links that have supported humans and beasts together in various regions in Africa. Pollock discusses many aspects of the continent's natural environment and history: pests and diseases, early hunters and gatherers, hunting and poaching today, human conflicts, expanding populations, agricultural needs, rituals, game farming, tourism, parks and game reserves, and conservation. Figures; maps; photographs; notes; index.

307. Potter, Van R. **Bioethics: Bridge to the Future.**
Englewood Cliffs, N.J.: Prentice-Hall, 1971. 205 p.

From a study of order and disorder in nature during his years in cancer research, Potter experienced a growing philosophical concern about the future and the human role in shaping it. He believes the concept of bioethics is the bridge between science and the humanities. Heretofore ethics have been limited to human relations; now we must recognize that human values cannot be separated from ecology. He credits a number of mentors with guiding his thought, among them Aldo Leopold, Margaret Mead, and Teilhard de Chardin. References at the end of each chapter; author and subject indexes.

308. ———. **Evolving Ethical Concepts.** Bio Science 27(4) April 1977: 251–253.

Following brief references to ethical concepts from the classics to the present, Potter provides a definition of "ethic" which, if applied, may avert ecological disaster.

309. **Power and Property in the Use of World Resources.** Celigny, Switzerland: World Council of Churches. 31 p.

Report of a consultation with economists, ecologists, and theologians at the Ecumenical Institute Bossey, April 20–25, 1974. Some thirty international participants concurred that "resources are the gifts of nature which first maintain human life, and, through the application of science, can increase man's opportunities for development." In his summary, Alain Blaney amplified this theme to include care of and respect for the environment and development to increase well-being of all while preserving this planet for future generations. A differing opinion came from Dr. A. M. Klaus-Miller, who predicted only catastrophe. The role of churches was also discussed.

310. Pringle, Lawrence. **The Only Earth We Have.** London: Collier-Macmillan, 1969. 86 p.

A textbook for fifth–eighth-grade students. It defines issues central to preserving the human environment. The text and photographs focus on situations in the United States, though some major world problems such as hunger are explored. Glossary and index.

311. Pryde, Philip R. **Conservation in the Soviet Union.** Cambridge, England: Cambridge University Press, 1972. 301 p.

While the preponderance of this book is concerned with practical measures for conservation and management of natural resources, it is based on an analysis of attitudes and values in the USSR. These include respect for nature and recognition of the need for ecological balance in the interest of this earth and its future inhabitants. Bibliography and index.

312. Quigg, P. W. **Habitat: Important Gains Despite Political Chaos.** Audubon 78(5) September 1976: 112–115.

Quigg describes the issues on which a consensus was reached at the United

Nations Conference in Vancouver in 1976. The natural environment figured importantly, and the Vancouver Symposium made significant contributions in this field. He also mentions some of the innovative techniques used at the Conference, especially audio-visual presentations.

313. Rasmussen, Larry L. **The Obsolescence of Conventional**
Deciding. Dialog 14(1) Winter 1975: 42–47.
A theologican posits that past norms and standards used in decision making have been outdated by relatively recent scientific knowledge; this information strongly indicates that the natural and human worlds are on a collision course. Never before have Christian ethicists had to make action choices on the basis of their responsibility to future generations as opposed to the present one. A new ethic is needed, less anthropocentric, more humble, and showing great restraint in our treatment of nature and in our own self-indulgence. Notes.

314. Ratcliffe, D. A. **Thoughts Toward a Philosophy of**
Nature Conservation. Biological Conservation 9(1) January
1976: 45–53.
Reflections of a British scientist and conservationist on some issues he confronted in constructing his own credo. He concentrates on concern for flora and fauna and their habitat; on this he based a personal ethic consistent with a wider interest for natural resources and humanity generally. His final note also reminds us to be aware of the magic of the natural world.

315. Raven, Charles E. **Natural Religion and Christian**
Theology. Cambridge, England: Cambridge University Press,
1953. 224 p.
The Gifford Lectures, 1951. A scholarly work on the subject from pre-biblical days to the present. The introduction, "Religion and Nature," poses the principal historical problems. Chapter II features several interpretations of early Hebrew and Greek attitudes toward nature. Chapters on the major Western cultural and scientific ages follow. Biblical references and notes.

316. Reed, Nathaniel P. **Compatible Environmental Change:**
A New Priority. Environmental Law 4(1) Fall 1973: 1–10.
Using land-use planning as a specific example, Reed shows how lawmakers and the public should recognize and accept the fact that we must live within the dictates of natural law. His concept of "compatible environmental change" is based on that position.

317. **Reflections on Theological Symbols, Man and Nature.**
Lutheran Quarterly 23(4) November 1971: 303–387.
The theme of the entire issue is "Religious Implications of the Ecological

Crisis." All of us are, as editor Daniel F. Martensen states, "novices when we look at the ecclesiastical, economic and political implications. . . ." The articles cover significant aspects of the problem. See especially Gilbert E. Doan, "Toward a Life Style Environmentally Informed." Other essays are by Myron Teske, Harold H. Ditmanson, R. Alvar Wargelin, and H. Paul Santmire; and a bibliography is by Douglas C. Stange.

318. Regan, Tom and Singer, Peter, eds. **Animal Rights and Human Obligations.** Englewood Cliffs, N.J.: Prentice-Hall, 1976. 250 p.
A galaxy of writers, both ancient and modern, present a range of views on humans' relations with other animals. Selected for the discussion they contain, the essays provoke a rethinking of moral and ethical concepts concerning current practices in the treatment of animals. Essays are by Thomas Aquinas, Aristotle, Descartes, Voltaire, Darwin, Schopenhauer, Schweitzer, Robert J. White, and the two editors, among others.

319. Reidel, Carl H. **Christianity and the Environmental Crisis.** Christianity Today 15(15) April 23, 1971: 4–8.
An interview in which, among other observations, Reidel stresses the destructive values of a society accustomed to ever-increasing technological affluence. He also challenges Lynn White's thesis on St. Francis of Assisi and refers, instead, to the New Testament parables and the admonitions concerning accumulation of material wealth. He suggests that it is time for Christians to practice what they preach.

320. Reveal, James L. and Broome, C. Rose. **Plant Rarity, Real and Imagined.** The Nature Conservancy News 29(2) March/April 1979: 4–8.
Two botanists define rarity and distinguish between natural extinctions and those caused by human activity. The latter they characterize as inexcusable and due chiefly to ignorance. Botanists should help to develop the emerging awareness of the innate worth of any organism.

321. Ripley, S. Dillon. **To Knit the Ravelled Sleeve. . .** *In* Smithsonian Year, 1978. Washington, D.C.: Smithsonian Institution, 1979. pp. 3–10.
In the preface to the Smithsonian Institution's annual report, this Secretary first discusses conservation in the museum, then transfers these thoughts into environmental conservation, which he believes is the ultimate responsibility and moral obligation for us all.

322. ———. **The Paradox of the Human Condition.** . . New
Delhi: Tata McGraw-Hill, 1975. 54 p.

Two lectures in the Sir Dorab Tata Memorial Lecture series. They comprise a scientific and historic survey of significant interactions of human groups in the world with their immediate environments; of past changes; and of modern problems. Ripley stresses the need for international co-operation on these matters. Increasingly societies are realizing that neither they nor the earth's biosphere can afford "careless technology." Ecological principles must evolve to guide and control needed technological innovation and must also be applied in societies that are careless about their population growth.

323. Ritschl, Dietrich. **Memory and Hope: An Inquiry Concerning the Presence of Christ.** New York: Macmillan, 1967. 237 p.

See especially section c) of chapter III, "The Enjoyment of God and the Separation of Nature and Grace." It contains an analysis of the roots of an important, Augustinian-based theme in Western theology which, in effect, degrades nature in order to affirm God.

324. Robinson, H. Wheeler. **Inspiration and Revelation in the Old Testament.** Oxford: Clarendon Press, 1946. 298 p.

A collection of discourses delivered at Oxford University by the Speaker's Lecturer, 1942–45. This scholarly work discusses the physical world as a manifestation of God. See especially part 1, "God and Nature." It also evaluates many other theological interpretations which have influenced both Judaism and Christianity. Scripture and subject index.

325. Rogers, Edward. **Plundered Planet.** Northfield, England: •
Denholm Press, 1973. 128 p.

After weighing the pros and cons of the ecological debate, Rogers feels that no valid conclusion can be reached without considering the nature and purpose of human existence. He explores the relevance of the doctrines of creation, stewardship, and judgment to the ecological situation. The environmental problem, he says, adds a practical element to theology; therefore modern theologicans must reexamine some of their presuppositions.

326. Rostand, Jean. **A Biologist's View.** London: Heinemann, 1956. 53 p.

Published first in French as "Ce que je crois," this essay expresses Rostand's beliefs as he approaches sixty years of age. He touches the great cosmic questions with humility and goes on to other reflections suggested by biological study. He sees differences between humans and other animals as quantitative in terms of thinking power, but qualitatively equal: he views the whole living world, from the microscopic to the human being, as a natural unity.

327. Roszak, Theodore. **Where the Wasteland Ends: Politics and Transcendence in Postindustrial Society.** Garden City, N.Y.: Doubleday, 1972. 492 p.

A far-ranging inquiry into some reasons for twentieth-century cultural alienation—a spiritual and political discontent that neither philosophical humanism nor dazzling technological achievements have been able to allay. Roszak is interested in the purposes and powers of ancient Middle-Eastern and Asian "magics," idolatries, and customs. He is highly critical of much in urban-industrial cultures, particularly that which contributes to distorted senses of reality among masses of people. The roles of science and religion are considered in the light of the enormous influence of the former upon modern life and the present possibility that religious renewal could resume equal influence in the future. Roszak elaborates his visionary polemic in the final chapters. Notes and asides.

328. Roueché, Berton. **What's Left: Reports on a Diminishing America.** Boston: Little, Brown, 1968. 210 p.

A record of trips of discovery to a variety of natural areas still intact in America and the attitudes and practices that threaten them. Conservation ethics in specific situations are contrasted with some opposing views.

329. Rubin, Louis D., and Kilpatrick, James J., eds. **The Lasting South: Fourteen Southerners Look at Their Home.** Chicago: Regnery, 1957. 208 p.

These writers address themselves to subjects identifying a southern individuality in the midst of transition. See especially James McB. Dabb's "The Land" on "the inner nature of Southern farming and its significance as a way of life"; Robert D. Jacob's "Woods and Water" on some motivations behind the modern breed of sports hunter; and Ellington White's "View from the Window" on technology and changing values.

330. Ruether, Rosemary. **Liberation Theology: Human Hope Confronts Christian History and American Power.** New York: Paulist Press, 1972. 194 p.

Ruether contends that a shift from some of the ancient beliefs in a holistic world occurred as moderns adapted to "civilized" doctrines. She posits that major economic systems foster "alienating" splits between humans and nature and between the sexes. Ruether suggests that such results may be traced historically to both the Christian and the preceding classical civilizations. See especially chapter 8, "Mother Earth and the Megamachine: A Theology of Liberation in a Feminine, Somatic and Ecological Perspective." Notes.

331. Rust, Eric C. **Nature and Man in Biblical Thought.**
London: Lutterworth Press, 1953. 318 p.
An investigation from a Christian viewpoint made as a "contribution to the problem of the philosophy of nature, which stands on the boundary between science and religion." See especially "The Conservation of Nature," in chapter IV and a discussion of the man-God-nature relationship as seen from early Christian and Hebrew outlooks in chapter V. Indexes.

332. ———. **Nature—Garden or Desert? An Essay on Environmental Theology.** Waco, Tex.: Word Books, 1971. 150 p.
A historical and philosophical look at the human relationship to nature and a plea to all persons rooted in the Judeo-Christian tradition to actively join others in saving the natural environment from further despoilment. Rust contends that this effort should contribute to new ethical developments disavowing selfishness, greed, and indifference. The church, he says, is sadly neglectful of this area of concern. Extensive notes.

333. Santmire, H. Paul. **Brother Earth: Nature, God and Ecology in Time of Crisis.** New York: Nelson, 1970. 236 p.
Presents clearly for a concerned public a historical view of the important dilemmas as well as some paradoxes manifest in the human relationship to nature, particularly in America. Santmire summarizes the several expressions of church teachings on nature. He also studies "the theology of nature" and of ideas which engender a vision of human responsibility.

334. Schaeffer, Francis A. **Pollution and the Death of Man: The Christian View of Ecology.** London: Hodder and Stoughton, 1970. 93 p.
Schaeffer uses Lynn White's "The Historical Roots of Our Ecological Crisis" and Richard Mean's "Why Worry about Nature?" to develop his own view that biblical Christianity has a viable answer to the ecological crisis. The Christian Church should teach that people can have dominion over nature without being destructive. Schaffer offers analysis of the two essays, in addition to his personal views.

335. Scheffer, Victor B. **Gallery of U. S. Animals in Peril Grows, But a New Wildlife Ethic is Emerging.** Photographs by Nina Leen. Smithsonian 4(7) October 1973: 45–51.
A portrait (in words and pictures) of a revolution in morality evolving from a human concern to care for all creatures.

336. Schilling, Harold K. **The New Consciousness in Science and Religion.** Philadelphia: Pilgrim Press, 1973. 288 p.

Schilling has distilled his own ideas and those of others to help people find a basis for faith in life, in nature, and in the "mysteries" of science. See especially, "Nature as a Source of Insight for Faith" and "Nature as a Source of Insight for Ethics—and about Sin." Notes and bibliography.

337. Schoenfeld, Clay. **Aldo Leopold Remembered.** Audubon 80 (3) May 1978: 28–37.

Schoenfeld's account of associations with and influence of Aldo Leopold. It concludes with a summary of the opinions Leopold might hold today were he alive and has many short quotes from lesser known writings which succinctly state his philosophy.

338. Schriver, Edward. **Leopold's Land Ethic: Wishful Thinking or Workable Dream?** Sierra Club Bulletin 62 (3) March 1977: 9–11, 16.

Schriver examines the scientific, economic, and behavioral objections to this ethic and concludes that, while its fulfillment is improbable, it is a dream worth attempting.

339. Schueler, Robert L. **Ecology—The New Religion?** America 122 (11) March 21, 1970: 292–295.

Referring to ecology as the "umbrella science" embracing biology, sociology, technology, and Christian humanism, this biologist writes of the human population problem as seen by the "new ecology." He finds acceptable middle ground between no control and total control to be Lynn White's approach via St. Francis of Assisi—less arrogance and more humility toward nature.

340. Schumacher, Ernest F. **Small is Beautiful: Economics as if People Mattered.** New York: Harper, 1973. 290 p.

Presents a challenge to the assumption that economic growth is desirable and necessary for satisfaction of human needs. Schumacher demonstrates that undirected growth has damaged the environment and debased humanity. He questions the philosophy of materialism and emphasizes instead the need for moral choices in decisions on the use of resources. See especially Buddhist economics (pp. 50–58) and references to other religions through the text; there is no index.

A posthumous work, "A Guide for the Perplexed," sums up Schumacher's religious beliefs and explores the route to a "good life" for those who find Western materialism unsatisfying.

341. Schweitzer, Albert. **The Teaching of Reverence for Life.** Translated [from the German] by Richard and Clara Winston. New York: Holt, 1965. 63 p.

Schweitzer weaves together the numerous threads which form the fabric of his personal philosophy of a reverence for all life, human and nonhuman. He concludes that a true spirit of humanitarianism must arise to counter modern moods of unconcern or cynicism.

342. Scott, Peter. **The Concern of the World Wildlife Fund and the Survival Service Commission with Threatened Wildlife in South East Asia.** *In* Conference on Conservation of Nature and Natural Resources in Tropical South East Asia, Bangkok, 1965. Proceedings. Morges, Switzerland: International Union for the Conservation of Nature and Natural Resources, 1968. pp. 38–39.

Brief report on how conservation organizations in Southeast Asia have responded to the conviction that threatened species must not be allowed to disappear. That imperative is based on ethical, aesthetic, scientific, and economic principles.

343. Sears, Paul B. **Beyond the Forest.** American Scientist 55(3) September 1967: 338–346.

A Sigma Xi-RESA Special National Lecture, Spring 1967. The lecturer shows how, in human societies, various concepts of value exist; one ethic is the conservation of natural resources. Sears then discusses the origin and growth of civilizations which are today unthinkingly destroying much of their environment.

344. ———. **Ethics, Aesthetics and the Balance of Nature.** *In* Perspectives on Conservation. Baltimore: Johns Hopkins Press, 1958. pp. 106–111.

From a Resources for the Future forum. Sears, an ecologist, stresses that society's choice is between a continually expanding economy, which is disastrous, and the return to a steady state based on biological reality. Other papers, such as those by John K. Galbraith and Philip M. Hauser, are also relevant.

345. Shahi, S. P. **Backs to the Wall: Saga of Wildlife in Bihar—India.** New Delhi: Affiliated East-West Press, 1977. 160 p.

Introduction by Salim Ali. This book by a noted forester of India's Bihar region was written to increase knowledge of India's fauna and to excite young people's enthusiasm to pursue careers in conservation. Shahi describes how very recent are serious efforts to save wildlife whose habitats are threatened by cultivation. Illustrated with Shahi's many color and black and white photographs. Bibliography.

346. Shepard, Paul. **Man in the Landscape: A Historic View of the Esthetics of Nature.** New York: Knopf, 1967. 290 p.
A sweeping study of the changing perceptions of nature in various cultural milieus from classical to modern. Shepard's imagery extends from wilderness to formal gardens, from nature-loving to nature-hating. He examines the animal-hunting syndrome and concepts of death and life in nature. Bibliography and index.

347. —— and McKinley, Daniel, eds. **The Subversive Science: Essays Toward an Ecology of Man.** Boston: Houghton, 1969. 453 p.
A collection of papers (some merely reprinted, some revised) on the theme that human health—physical, mental, spiritual—requires a healthy environment. See especially the introduction: "Ecology and Man—a Viewpoint"; "God's Acre" by Erich Isaac; and "Ethos, Ecos and Ethics." Bibliographies at the end of some papers; additional readings.

348. ——. **Thinking Animals and the Development of Human Intelligence.** New York: Viking, 1978. 274 p.
Much of this book is devoted to demonstrating how animals and our associations with them are essential to the human mind. Shepard argues that animals are neither economically nor ecologically necessary and that humans are too imperfect for ethics to prevail in their conduct toward other animals, especially when both are competing for the same space.

349. Shepherd, J. Barrie. **Theology for Ecology.** The Catholic World 211 (1264) July 1970: 172–175.
Society's efforts to deal with ecological crisis cannot succeed without a "totally new attitude" which in religious terms is a "theology for ecology." Shepherd mentions medieval Christian emphasis on "this barren land" and suggests instead that we go back to the Bible and retrieve the concept of the world as God's creation—the same vision in Old and New Testaments.

350. Sherrell, Richard E., ed. **Ecology: Crisis and New Vision.** Richmond, Va.: John Knox Press, 1970. 159 p.
A collection of ten essays by theologians (Jewish, Christian, and a student of Zen Buddhism), a philosopher, an educator, and a professor of natural resources. The collection resulted from efforts to carry knowledge of the ecological crisis toward a search for a new vision that will assist humans in making responsible social decisions. Such decisions involve the affluent and the poor, military and political power groups, scientists, and all who

recognize the need for new, creative, and more humane technologies. Notes.

351. Simmons, I. G. **Wilderness in the Mid-Twentieth Century U. S. A.** Town Planning Review 36(4) January 1966: 249–256.

An Englishman analyzes the situation in the United States and concludes that here, as in England, population must be controlled and the quality of urban life improved to preserve any natural areas. It is essential to provide not only recreation but some untouched and unreachable places for both scientific benefit and spiritual satisfaction.

352. Simonds, John O. **Earthscape: A Manual of Environmental Planning.** New York: McGraw, 1978. 340 p.

This book is intended as a basic primer of practical principles which are, in turn, dependent on scientific, cultural, and philosophical precepts; on new interest in the relationships of people; and on the natural world and concern for the future. The text occupies the center of the page with appropriate quotes and illustrations in the margins. There are also full-page illustrations, a subject index, and an index of quotation sources.

353. Singer, Peter. **Animal Liberation: A New Ethics for Our Treatment of Animals.** New York: New York Review; distributed by Random House, 1975. 301 p.

This philosopher believes that the basic moral principle of equality should apply to all sentient beings. The book describes the suffering caused by human tyranny over other animals and suggests remedies. Chapter V, "Man's Dominion," is especially pertinent.

See the critique by Michael Fox and reply by Tom Regan in Ethics 88(2) January 1978: 126–138.

354. Sittler, Joseph. **Ecological Commitment as Theological Responsibility.** Zygon 5(2) June 1970: 172–181; Idoc (9) September 12, 1970: 76–85.

Addresses at the John XXIII Institute Conference on Theology and Ecology, St. Xavier College, Chicago, January 31, 1970 and the World Council of Churches Exploratory Conference on Technology and the Future of Man and Society, Geneva, June 28–July 4, 1970. Sittler offers a series of proposals: first, that the question of reality is itself an ecological question; second, that nature's objects should be regarded in the original sense of "behold"; third, that a study of being leads to thinking about relations between God and humans. Each of these is treated by analysis of biblical statements and leads to the conclusion that the doctrine of grace is the link between ecology and theology.

355. ———. **Essays on Nature and Grace.** Philadelphia:
Fortress Press, 1972. 134 p.
These six essays address in fresh ways the biblical ideas of redemption
and grace. Sittler's study clarifies in both the historical and ecumenical
senses the concepts of nature and God's concern for the total creation.
In the final chapter, "Christian Theology and the Environment," he discusses the complexity of decision making today and suggests that we must
have a "gracious" understanding and joyful appreciation of earth's gifts
lest we abuse them.

356. ———. **A Theology For Earth.** The Christian Scholar
37(3) September 1954: 367–374.
An essay on the "matter of the relation of Christian faith and nature";
it is a chiding answer to Reinhold and Richard Niebuhr, Richard Kroner,
John Bennett, and others whose orthodox reading of the relation of Christianity to culture omits a "theology for Earth." Three possible relationships between humans and the natural world are given. Sittler concludes
that Christian theology must finally articulate and infuse into its teachings
the true meaningfulness of the world of nature.

357. Skutch, Alexander P. **Meditations of a Naturalist.**
Nature Magazine.
Contents: **The Root of the Evil** 37(9) November 1944: 466–468; **Back-or
Forward-to Nature** 39(9) November 1946: 457–460, 498; **Our Difficult
Choice** 47(4) April 1954: 190–192, 215; **The Tangled Strands of Conservation**
47(5) May 1954: 258–260, 276.
From his partial retirement in Central America, a noted scientist reflects
on the human and the natural world. In the concluding article of the series
he finds the religious or ethical motive for conservation (which he traces
to the oldest beliefs of both East and West) the only valid one to follow.

358. Slusser, Dorothy M. and Slusser, Gerald H.
Technology—The God That Failed. Philadelphia:
Westminister Press, 1971. 169 p.
By responding to material desires from the wealthiest quarter of the world,
science and technology seem to be on a runaway course that is seriously
eroding the environment. Discussions of population pressures, agri-business' industrial farming techniques, and ecocide are followed by a brief
summary of some past and present visions that may foster a religious
regard (not in the institutional sense) for the "aliveness of nature."

359. Small, George L. **The Blue Whale.** New York:
Columbia University Press, 1971. 248 p.
A case study on the blue whale, slaughtered by man to near extinction.
Small describes the tragedy of the blue whale as a reflection of a greater

tragedy—that of the human race. He asks: "How long will man persist in the belief that he is the master of this earth and not one of its guests? . . . Survival chances for the human race will be greatly enhanced when man concedes to Earth and all its life forms the right to exist that he wants for himself."

360. Smith, Anthony W. **The Profit Motive and the Environment.** National Parks and Conservation Magazine 46 (1) January 1972: 21–24.

Address by the President of the National Parks and Conservation Association before the Conservation Committee of the Garden Clubs of America, New York, October 12, 1971. Smith notes that modern corporations are, in effect, social institutions and that it behooves their managers to develop a social conscience and work with environmentalists to help industries function on a sound ecological and humanitarian basis; otherwise they will be regulated and restricted. He suggests that garden-club women are in a particularly good position to stimulate such a philosophy in business.

361. ———. **Splendor in the Parks.** EPA Journal 5(6) June 1979: 16–17, 26.

Review of the national parks which were set aside to preserve specimens of our natural heritage and to symbolize a fruitful relationship between humans and nature.

362. Smith, Lewis G. **Towards a Pro-Life Society.** Boston: Branden Press, 1975. 142 p.

Smith defines a pro-life society as a combination of conservatism, liberalism, and humanism. Chapter 4, "Structuring a Pro-Life Environment," envisions: regional land-use planning that would cross state lines; nucleonic population dispersion rather than crowded cities; population control through education to build new sexual mores; cooperation rather than competition; and an ultimate changeover "from a non-value-based money system to an inanimate energy-based system, probably solar." He admits that these proposals are long-range (maybe 1000 years); in the meantime conservation is the key word.

363. Smith, Robert L. **The Ecology of Man: An Ecosystem Approach.** 2d ed. New York: Harper, 1976. 399 p.

An overview of human ecology which serves as a textbook for courses dealing with humans and their environment. The introduction to each section provides the text and commentaries; selections from different authors present varying or expanded views. See especially "Man's Attitude Toward Nature," which briefly explores Judeo-Christian beliefs, oriental philosophies, and American Indian cultures and concludes there is essentially no difference among their attitudes toward nature. These beliefs are reinforced by René Dubos' "Judeo-Christian Attitudes," which points out that human activities started affecting nature 10,000 years before the Bible was written and suggests that if there is any reverence or concern for nature, it is to be found in the Bible. References accompany each paper; additional "Selected References"; index.

364. **The Social Costs of Energy Choices.** Christianity and Crisis 38(15) October 16, 1978: 238–252.

This issue examines the components of energy decisions. The editors of this journal believe the focus of the debate on energy production and use should be changed to emphasize how decisions will affect everybody, including the unborn. Ethics should be part of the decision making process. Three of the articles deal with specific human problems: poverty, health, and employment. The other two examine the development of ecological justice.

365. South Pacific Conference on National Parks and Reserves, 1975, Wellington, N. Z. **Proceedings. . .** Sponsored by the New Zealand Government in association with the South Pacific Commission and the International Union for the Conservation of Nature and Natural Resources. Wellington: Dept. of Lands and Survey, 1975. 299 p.

The theme of this conference was preservation of the environment by "people who care . . . for themselves, their neighbors and those who come after them." Speakers referred to the: need for beauty, stewardship concept, beliefs of the original inhabitants, as well as practical political and economic measures for setting aside national parks and reserves.

366. Spring, David and Spring, Eileen, eds. **Ecology and Religion in History.** New York: Harper, 1974. 154 p.

A collection of seven celebrated and often controversial essays beginning with Lynn White's "The Historical Roots of Our Ecologic Crisis." Others are John Macquarrie, "Creation and Environment"; James Barr, "Man and Nature: the Ecological Controversy and the Old Testament"; Lewis W. Moncrief, "The Cultural Basis for Our Environmental Crisis"; Yi-Fu Tuan, "Discrepancies Between Environmental Attitude and Behavior: Examples from Europe and China"; René Dubos, "Franciscan Conservation Versus Benedictine Stewardship"; and Arnold Toynbee, "The Religious Background of the Present Environmental Crisis." Bibliography.

367. Sprout. Harold and Sprout, Margaret. **The Ecological Perspective on Human Affairs. . .** Princeton: Princeton University Press, 1965. 236 p.

An expansion of a 1956 essay by the Sprouts entitled "Man-milieu Relationship Hypotheses in the Context of International Politics," which stimulated great reader comment. Here they examine critically the practical use of environmental concepts and theories in the analysis and formulation of international policies. They conclude that "more general awareness of the intellectual, . . . moral and civic consequences of ecological terms . . . and theories . . . could contribute to more precise and enlightening explanations and predictions of human behavior and achievement."

368. Stacey, W. David. **The Christian View of Nature.** The
Expository Times 67(12) September 1956: 364–367.
Stacey tries to answer some of the questions that confuse Christians. He studies the creation, the relation of nature to God, and the place of nature in the redemption of humanity. He makes specific reference to the Bible and to several theologians, principally C. S. Lewis.

369. Starkloff, Carl F. **American Indian Religion and
Christianity: Confrontation and Dialogue.** Journal of
Ecumenical Studies 8(2) Spring 1971: 317–340.
An unromanticized description of the advanced theological monotheism of the Arapaho Indians of Wyoming. While these Native Americans are receptive to the teachings of Christ, Starkloff proposes that Christians have even more to learn from the Arapaho culture which is sensitive to the obligations of community living and cooperation and is advanced in the "poetry of religious expression, joy in creation, reverence for all things. . . ." Notes.

370. Starr, Kevin. **Robinson Jeffers and the Integrity of
Nature.** Sierra Club Bulletin 62(5) May 1977: 36–40.
A scholar discovers in the poet's life and writings a philosophy of creation as the sound beginning of an environmental ethic.

371. Steffenson, Dave. **Beyond Survival.** Journal of
Environmental Education 6(3) Spring 1975: 7–9.
The Campus Minister of the University of Wisconsin-Green Bay reviews the opinions of various thinkers in search of a new environmental ethic that will offer a more positive value than "survival." References.

372. Stefferud, Alfred, ed. **Christians and the Good Earth.**
[New York] Published by Friendship Press for the Faith-
Man-Nature Group, 1969. 190 p. (F/M/N Papers No. 1)
Talks and discussions at the Third National Conference of the Group, 1967. Theologians, civil servants, scientists, and officials of conservation organizations debate conservation, preservation, and restoration of a habitable planet. Subjects include development of "An Ecological Conscience for America," "The Role of the Church," action strategies, and a contemporary view of humankind's relation to nature.

373. —— and Nelson, Arnold L., eds. **Birds in Our Lives.**
Illustrated by Bob Hines. Washington, D. C.: U. S. Govt.
Print. Off., 1966. 561 p.

A compilation undertaken by the Fish and Wildlife Service. Fifty-four
chapters contributed by well-known writers give a wide perspective on
birds as they affect and are affected by people and other forms of life.
For a discussion of ethics, see the foreword by Stewart L. Udall, then
Secretary of the Interior, and many individual chapters such as "What
Are Birds For?" by Roger T. Peterson; "Mark What You Leave," by
Roland C. Clement; "A Conservationist's View" by Clarence Cottam;
and others. Neither "ethics" nor "conservation" appears in the index.

374. Steidle, Edward. **A Philosophy for Conservation.** College
Station: Pennsylvania State College, School of Mineral
Industries, 1949. 52 p. (Mineral Industries Experiment State
Circular #33) (Pennsylvania State College Bulletin v. 43,
no. 6)

Steidle states that the human attitude or character must change soon in
order to deal with increasing consumer demands for finite raw materials.
He also says that while legal enforcement of industrial practices is necessary, even more important is the "expansion of basic fundamental research." Other chapters cover human resources, human discord and
greed, and industrial raw materials.

375. Steiger, Brad. **Medicine Power: the American Indian's
Revival of his Spiritual Heritage and its Relevance for Modern
Man.** Garden City, N. Y.: Doubleday, 1974. 226 p.

A collection of episodes, conversations, and stories illustrating the resurgence of American Indian philosophy and religion. The emphasis is on
peace, love, and harmony with neighbors, nature, and the universe. The
final chapter "Walk in Balance" pleads for all people to obey the laws
of nature.

376. Stivers, Robert L. **The Sustainable Society: Ethics and
Economic Growth.** Philadelphia: Westminster Press, 1976.
240 p.

Stivers analyzes our modern, growth-oriented society in the context of
Christian ethics. He posits that we exploit nature, we succumb to a "religion of growth," and we divorce spiritual values from economic activity.
He concludes that contemporary Western society needs a new world view
or ethic and a new set of priorities. Bibliographic notes.

377. Stone, Christopher D. **Should Trees Have Standing?
Toward Legal Rights for Natural Objects.** Foreword by

Garrett Hardin. Los Altos, Calif.: William Kaufmann, 1974. 102 p.

The first chapters constitute a philosophical essay on how recognition of our responsibilities as trustees of the earth can be translated into effective legal principles. The concluding section reprints the opinions and dissents of the Supreme Court in the Mineral King case.

378. Stone, Glen C., ed. **A New Ethic for a New Earth.** [New York] Published by Friendship Press for Faith-Man-Nature Group and the National Council of Churches, 1971. 176 p.

Papers presented at the Group's Fourth National Conference, 1969. Participants include ecologists, biologists, and theologians. There is a preface by Senator Gaylord Nelson and a concluding resolution dealing with the problems of population growth and depletion of natural resources, topics with which the conference was principally concerned. On the future environment, see especially Frederick Elder's "A Different 2001" and Roger Theobald's "The Changing Environment: Does the Church Have a Major Responsibility?" Bibliography.

379. Storer, John H. **The Web of Life: A First Book of Ecology.** New York: Devin Adair, 1953. 142 p.

An explanation of the operation of the natural world, with its complex, interdependent patterns of living things. It shows the natural community in action, all parts functioning, and argues for wise use and enlightened management of soil, water, minerals, forests, and wildlife. Photographs.

380. Storm, Hyemeyohsts. **Seven Arrows.** New York: Harper, 1972. 371 p.

A narrative that explains some of the lessons and ancient wisdom of the Plains Indians—the Cheyenne, the Crow, and the Sioux. Legends and tales included reveal that by caring for the earth and trying to understand the forms and cycles of life a person or whole group can learn to tolerate vicissitudes and to know gratitude for the gift of life.

381. Strickland, Rennard. **Environmental Essay: Puritan, Indian, and Agrarian. . .** St. Mary's Law Journal 3, 1971: 231–248.

An in-depth review of the book "Puritanism and the Wilderness: The Intellectual Significance of the New England Frontier, 1629–1700," by Peter N. Carroll (New York: Columbia University Press, 1969).

The reviewer presents two divergent historical attitudes toward the human relationship with nature: those of New England Puritans, steeped in biblical traditions, and those of American Indians, particularly the Cherokees. Their influences are explored.

382. Strong, Douglas H. and Rosenfeld, Elizabeth S. **Ethics or Expediency: An Environmental Question.** Environmental Affairs 5(2) Spring 1976: 255–270.

Noting that the future depends on present-day decision making, the authors examine two ethical systems which have molded present society to see how they can be improved. The first is the Judeo-Christian; the second they call the pragmatic-utilitarian. They find both systems lacking and call for a more clearly defined ethical principle, searching through the ideas of Paul Shepard, Aldo Leopold, and other philosophers. They conclude that enlightened self-interest can form the basis for an effective environmental ethic.

383. Swan, Christopher and Roaman, Chet. **YV88: An Eco-Fiction of Tomorrow.** San Francisco: Sierra Club, 1977. 248 p.

An imaginary first step out of the age of grandiose technology and commercial sprawl. The prototype is Yosemite Valley in the 1980s. The aim is to show some kinds of technology that integrate natural energy sources and human labor with the natural life of the planet. Created in this vision is a totally humane environment, uncluttered, convenient, and welcoming to wilderness seekers and others, both human and wild. Obstacles and frustrations are anticipated, but the possibilities could be catching!

384. Szent-Gyorgyi, Albert. **The Crazy Ape: Written by a Biologist for the Young.** New York: Philosophical Library, 1970. 93 p.

Presents some moral, economic, and political paradoxes in modern America, with ramifications that extend to the rest of the world. The central question is: Will humanity be able to survive the violence and turbulence of this age of transition or will we, doubting reverence for life and creation, continue to act too often like "crazy apes?"

385. ———. **Knowledge, Intelligence and Their Sane Use.** Impact of Science on Society 22(4) October-December 1972, 315–328.

Adapted from an interview originally reported in "New Hungarian Quarterly." This Nobel Prize-winning scientist sums up his belief that the pursuit and application of scientific knowledge should be governed by respect for one another and wise use of natural resources.

386. ———. **What Next?!** New York: Philosophical Library, 1971. 68 p.

Brief recapitulation of some of the points in "The Crazy Ape" with suggestions for solutions to the problems iterated. It is addressed to youth, who, the author believes, can establish new goals and priorities and create a world based on moral, ethical, and spiritual values.

387. **Taking Charge: Achieving Personal and Political Change Through Simple Living.** The Simple Living Collective, American Friends Service Committee, San Francisco. New York: Bantam, 1977. 341 p.

A book containing questions and views on the "whys" and "hows" of community living, directed to Americans who would like to live more harmoniously with the environment and the rest of the world family. These same people may be uneasy knowing that six percent of the earth's population—the United States—consumes over a third of its natural resources. *Taking Charge* includes information and action guides for changes in political and economic power, locally, nationally, and internationally. It concludes with the Shakertown Pledge, the introduction and first commitment of which concerns the idea of stewardship and an ecologically sound way of life. Study aids and bibliographies at the end of each chapter.

388. Taylor, Gordon R. **The Doomsday Book.** London: Thames and Hudson, 1970. 235 p.

Taylor brings together much of the material, experiences, and gloomy predictions of previous environmentalists and presents a poignant picture of the environmental crisis as he found it in 1970. Looking to the future, he concludes that we find ourselves in a threefold crisis of: values or how we *ought* to live; disconnectedness—society is too large, hence too impersonal and unrelated; and responsibility.

389. Taylor, Richard, K. **Economics and the Gospel: A Primer on Shalom as Economic Justice.** Philadelphia: United Church Press, 1973. 125 p.

The Shalom Curriculum is based upon ethical principles that encourage cooperative living among families and communities so that, in terms of Western societies, there is minimum impact upon earth's natural resources. Its references are common to Christian-Judaic teachings. See especially pp. 100–116.

390. Teilhard de Chardin, Pierre. **The Phenomenon of Man.** With an introduction by Sir Julian Huxley. New York: Harper, 1959. 318 p.

By uniting the great purposes of science and religion the human race may realize a converging harmony with all God's natural works on this planet and in the universe. The "phenomenon" of man is not that he is the "static centre of the world," but rather that he has within him the seed of understanding which may enable him eventually to comprehend the unity of divine creation. The philosophical ramifications of the works of this scientist-priest have influenced the thinking of scientists, theologians, and many others who are concerned with environmental ethics. Appendix and index.

391. Terry, Mark. **Hello Ents, Good-Bye Aristotle.** Natural
History 80(1) January 1971: 6–22.
A biology teacher describes a new way of looking at everyday things: a typewriter's plastic parts as a toxic concentration of formerly beneficial carbons; paper, the heart of a stand of trees; and copper coins, the ripped off side of a mountain. He then goes on to describe the results of our consumption-growth philosophy and concludes with precepts which can be used in environmental education.

392. Thomas, Lewis. **The Lives of a Cell: Notes of a Biology
Watcher.** New York: Viking, 1974. 153 p.
As biologist, doctor, and philosopher, Thomas is continually startled by the remarkable complexity and toughness of life in all its forms. He doubts human dominance or endurance in the long pull unless we realize how interlocked we are with the rest of creation and get over the idea of being overlords, superior and apart. Reference notes.

393. Tilden, Freeman. **Riches of Being: The Century Since
Yellowstone.** National Parks and Conservation Magazine
46(1) January 1972: 4–9.
A member of the National Park Service reviews the developments and recognition of a land ethic which brings what he calls "the riches of being" as opposed to the "riches of having."

394. **To Love or to Perish: The Technological Crisis and the
Churches.** Edited by Edward Carothers and others. New
York: Friendship Press, 1972. 152 p.
A report of the U. S. Task Force on the Future of Mankind in a World of Science-Based Technology, co-sponsored by the National Council of the Churches of Christ and the Union Theological Seminary of New York. The report consists of position papers selected by the group. The first, "A Manifesto for Tomorrow," states the theme that to save the earth and its peoples we must seek a less materialistic life style and have respect for our neighbors. The concluding section is a discussion on the role of the churches in implementing the "Manifesto."

395. Toynbee, Arnold. **The Religious Background of the
Present Environmental Crisis: A Viewpoint.** International
Journal of Environmental Studies 3(2) May 1972: 141–146.
The historian points to a few major, disastrous effects of the technological evolution in this century. The pre-Industrial-Revolution spirit of scientific

inquiry was based largely upon political and social considerations, yet industrial development itself encouraged human greed and a disregard for nature. Toynbee questions the validity of monotheistic religions which teach a concept of a "unique God who is super-human in power, . . ." but which neglect the "rights of nature." He asserts that in both pre-Christian Greek and Latin literature and in most Asian religions the awe of nature generated a healthy respect. He conjectures that one possible remedy for environmental outrages is philosophical reversion to pantheism and Eastern religions.

396. Trefethen, James B. **An American Crusade for Wildlife.** Rev. ed. Drawings by Peter Corbin. New York: Winchester Press and the Boone and Crockett Club, 1975. 409 p.

Originally conceived as a history of the Boone and Crockett Club and its relation to the evolution of enlightened concepts and practices among hunters, the book became a history of the conservation movement since 1887, when Theodore Roosevelt founded the Club. Trefethen delineates the evolution of laws and regulations and how they were made, the growth and direction of government agencies, and the founding of the major conservation organizations. Focusing on wildlife conservation and management, he traces environmental philosophy in this century. Through incidents and case histories he characterizes the attitudes of contrasting interest groups. Appendix of common and scientific names of birds and mammals mentioned in the text; references.

397. Tuan, Yi-Fu. **Man and Nature.** Washington, D.C.: Association of American Geographers, 1971. 49 p. (Resource Paper No. 10)

One of the series developed by the Commission on College Geography supplementing existing texts on topics of importance in modern geography. An attempt to reach a philosophical understanding of the theme through condensation of ideas contributed by philosophers, scientists (both physical and social) and humanists. After providing definitions, Tuan presents views of "Man as a Biological Organism" and "Man as an Agent for Change." Then he studies spatial and social relationships with a separate chapter on "The Population Dilemma." He criticizes the modern concepts of environmentalism and ecology, but apparently believes these have supplanted religion in human thinking. Extensive bibliography.

398. Tunnard, Christopher. **A World With a View: An Inquiry into the Nature of Scenic Values.** New Haven: Yale University Press, 1978. 196 p.

Concerned with the lack of an aesthetic conscience in planning, Tunnard discusses the value of landscape. For both scientific and aesthetic reasons he urges scenic preservation in some areas and careful consideration of use of the land in all development. He illustrates his point with paintings by famous artists. Bibliographic notes and index of names.

399. Turner, Ernest S. **Dominion Over the Beasts.** *In* his All Heaven in a Rage. New York: St. Martins, 1964. pp. 16–27.
Condensed history of philosophical, religious, and humanistic attitudes towards animals from ancient Greek and Roman times through the Renaissance.

400. Udall, Stewart L. **The Quiet Crisis.** Introduction by John F. Kennedy. New York: Holt, 1963. 209 p.
Udall, then Secretary of the Interior, prepared this outline of this continent's history and people to convince Americans of the need for stewardship of the lands they were given. It begins with "The Land Wisdom of the Indians" and continues to ". . . a Land Ethic for Tomorrow." Illustrated with numerous photographs. Acknowledgments; bibliographic notes and index.

401. **The Unfinished Agenda: The Citizen's Policy Guide to Environmental Issues.** Edited by Gerald O. Barney. New York: Crowell, 1977. 184 p.
A task force report (sponsored by the Rockefeller Brothers Fund) representing a consensus of America's leading environmental thinkers, who identify and treat priority issues for the coming decade. While the book has specific chapters on population, food and agriculture, energy, natural resources, water and air pollution, toxic substances, land use, and biological threats, it emphasizes the interrelatedness of all of these. The work concludes with chapters on values, society, and decision making. There is an outline of the need for, and possibilities in, national planning. Notes and index.

402. United Nations Conference on the Human Environment, Stockholm, 1972. **Report.** New York: United Nations, 1973. 17 p. (Document. A/CONF/14/Rev.1)
Official report of the first world conference on the environment. Especially important is the Declaration of Principles, whose preamble proclaims that "Man is both creature and moulder of his environment which gives him physical sustenance and affords him the opportunity for intellectual, moral, social, and spiritual growth . . ." and that "The natural resources of the earth . . . must be safeguarded for the benefit of present and future generations."

Pre-conference documents and the Non-Governmental Organizations declaration should be consulted for full discussion of the moral responsibility of humans toward the environment and toward each other.

403. U. S. Dept. of the Interior. **Living With Our
Environment.** Washington, D.C.: U.S. Govt. Print. Off.,
1978. 120 p. (Conservation Yearbook No. 12)
Latest annual report on the conservation activities of the Department.
Throughout there are many references to philosophy and ethics in environmental decision making. For example, Cecil Andrus suggests that now
is certainly the time to strive for spiritual riches rather than the former
"American dream" of material wealth. See also the sections on Alaska;
and "One Man's Environment" by M. Woodbridge Williams. Illustrated
with many color photographs.

404. Van den Bosch. Robert. **The Pesticide Conspiracy.**
Garden City, N.Y.: Doubleday, 1978. 226 p.
A professor of entomology documents the case the public has against most
of the agricultural-chemical industry, as well as a consortium of pesticide-
related businesses and political, economic, and professional groups. These
powerful interests control much agricultural research and have important
political connections. Van den Bosch outlines steps to achieve integrated
pest-management systems using a combination of biological controls and
safe, selected pesticides. He is not optimistic that human health and ecological stability will win this battle very soon, given the prevailing economic and political climate in America today. Preface by Paul R. Ehrlich.
Glossary; notes; bibliography.

405. Vanstone, William H. **On the Being of Nature.** Theology
80(676) July 1977: 279–283.
Expounds the personal philosophy of a growing number of people that
other living or non-living things of the earth have intrinsic worth aside
from whether or not they are seen as of any possible service to humans.
This "new kind of reverence" presents many problems, but Vanstone
writes that it is an area deserving serious theological reflection.

406. Vaux, Kenneth. **Subduing the Cosmos: Cybernetics and
Man's Future.** Richmond, Va.: John Knox Press, 1970.
197 p.
The human being "is meant" to subdue the environment of earth and
beyond. This mandate to God's co-worker entails value considerations.
Vaux reflects on "the ethical significance of electric technology and man's
use of that power to control environment." Extensive notes and
bibliography.

407. Vogt, William. **Road to Survival.** New York: Sloane,
1948. 335 p.
One of the earliest of the books calling attention to incipient disaster due
to misuse of the earth and its resources, war, and overpopulation. He

101

believes the United States must lead the way in reorienting the lives and thinking of people all over the world; that we must recognize that we all make the problem; and that we must learn our place in the universe before we begin seeking for solutions. References; reading lists; subject index.

408. Vorspan, Albert. **The Crisis of Ecology: Judaism and the Environment.** *In* his Jewish Values and Social Crisis. New York: Union of American Hebrew Congregations, 1970. pp. 179–198.

After a brief analysis of the existing deteriorated state of the environment, Vorspan summarizes from biblical sources the Jewish belief in the stewardship of nature and respect for other human beings. Lists of readings, films, and music; sources for further information.

409. Wagner, Philip L. **The Human Use of the Earth.** Glencoe, Ill.: The Free Press, 1960. 270 p.

A geographer examines functions of both artificial and natural environments in human culture. The book is designed to help fill the gap that often divides social sciences from physical and biological sciences. Many human cultures and social arrangements are examined in light of geographical and ecological themes revolving around the observation that "man is inherently a restless remaker of his own world." Extensive notes and index.

410. Wald, George. **Decision and Destiny: The Future of Life on Earth.** Zygon 5(2) June 1970: 159–171.

A professor of biology at Harvard discusses his view of the universe. He includes John T. Needham's interpretation of the creation as recorded in Genesis, that God did not actually make living creatures but ordered the earth and the waters to produce them; therefore it was spontaneous generation. Wald also discusses technological and biological design. He cites the principle of natural selection and points to Darwin as the first to realize that this principle applies to all aspects of human society—politics, social problems, aesthetics, ethics, conflict, and competition. He concludes with several actions which must be taken to preserve life on this planet.

Ward, Barbara: see Jackson, Barbara (Ward) *Lady*

411. Warden, Alastair N. **Man, Animal and the Environment, Especially in Wales.** International Journal of Environmental Studies 7(2) 1975: 107–117.

Edited lecture at the University College of Wales, Aberstwyth, November 28, 1973. A discussion of the environmental problems of Wales with frequent reference to the ethical aspects of solutions. References.

412. Waters, Frank. **Pumpkin Seed Point.** Chicago: Sage, 1969. 175 p.

A personal narrative of years spent among Indians of the Southwestern United States and Mexico and of some of the conflicts in values and beliefs between the red and white peoples that Waters encounters. See especially "Two Views of Nature." Glossary.

413. Watts, Alan W. **Nature, Man and Woman.** New York: Vintage, 1970. 209 p.

A philosophical exploration of problems central to human association with nature. Asian and Western attitudes are compared, including those affecting the man-woman relationship. Chapter 2, "Science and Nature," contains a discussion of traditional Christian and Asian attitudes toward nature; the Western attempt to adjust nature through science and technology is compared to Hindu cosmology. Bibliographical references.

414. Weeden, Robert B. **Technology and Wildlife.** Technology Review 78(1) October/November 1973: 38–45.

A professor of wildlife management discusses the environmental value questions arising from recognition of interdependence in the universe and the decisions which must be made because of increases in population and technology.

415. Westman, W. E. **How Much Are Nature's Services Worth?** Science 197 (4307) September 2, 1977: 960–964.

Using examples, this ecologist concludes that cost-benefit analyses applied to cases of disturbance and/or restoration of ecosystem balances are inadequate for decision making because they consistently skew estimates of nature's value.

416. **What Good Are Endangered Species Anyway? On Taxes and Lettuce** by David Ehrenfeld; **On Esthetics and Honor** by Henry Mitchell. National Parks and Conservation Magazine 52 (10) October 1978: 10–12.

Two articles emphasizing that while humans may be tempted, they do not have the intrinsic right to decide which species shall live and which shall be eliminated. Mitchell also states that the decision we make influences our conduct toward other people and our own self-regard.

417. **When Values Conflict: Essays on Environmental Analysis, Discourse and Decision.** Edited by Laurence H. Tribe, Corinne S. Schelling, and John Voss. Cambridge, Mass.: Ballinger, 1976. 179 p.

A group appointed by the American Academy of Arts and Sciences and representing disciplines in the natural and social sciences authored these essays, which resulted from their discussions. Their initial task was to investigate the feasibility of establishing a national environmental research institute to guide decision makers. They were also to decide how such an institution could include and make effective such "fragile" values as wilderness and preservation of species in comparison with "hard" values such as cost-effectiveness and employment. Their discussions changed their emphasis into a study of how to resolve value conflicts. They interacted with a group studying the Tocks Island Dam controversy as an example of a live, environmental issue with conflicting value components. The essays in this volume illustrate the philosophies of the various participants. For some, values must be based on a moral conception of humanity in relation to nature. Others think that each situation should be studied separately without any basic commitment. Notes at the end of each essay; subject index.

418. White, Elwyn B. **The Morning of the Day They Did It.** *In* his The Second Tree from the Corner. New York: Harper, 1954. pp. 52–70.

————. **Sootfall and Fallout.** *In* his The Points of My Compass. New York: Harper, 1962. pp. 77–89.
The first of these essays is a fantasy of the last days of Earth and how it is destroyed by human greed and ineptitude. The second is a description and condemnation of nuclear power. Both are representative of White's concern with an environmental ethic.

419. White, Hugh C., ed. **Christians in a Technological Era.** New York: Seabury Press, 1964. 143 p.
A collection of essays examining the relation between religion (especially Christianity) and the modern technological society. In her introduction, Margaret Mead analyzes the dynamics of each, with emphasis on the responsibility of one generation to the next to ensure the survival of life on earth.

420. White, Lynn. **The Historical Roots of Our Ecologic Crisis.** Science 155(3767) March 10, 1967: 1203–1207.
Traces the historical development of the idea of perpetual human and material progress rooted in Judeo-Christian teachings, which established a dualism between man and nature as God's will. White suggests that religious education should be re-directed to more humble attitudes, such as those espoused by St. Francis of Assisi.

421. Whitehouse, W. A. **Toward a Theology of Nature.** Scottish Journal of Theology 17(2) June 1964: 129–145.
Whitehouse discusses the changing connotations of the term "nature" in

order to enlarge upon the possibilities open to the modern theologian for speaking of the physical world as deserving of wonder and reverence. The question is how to articulate these aspects of "revelation." This article aims to clear the way for a supportable, modern vision. Notes.

422. Whyte, William H. **The Last Landscape.** Garden City, N.Y.: Doubleday, 1968. 376 p.

In Whyte's view, an environmental ethic applies to more than just to the saving of unspoiled natural areas. As cities take over more of the land and comprise humanity's chief habitat, our recognition of the role of the laws of nature must be applied here too. He outlines practical ways for evolving urban areas to conform with our best standards of a harmonious society in tune with nature. There are specific case histories and concepts by the man responsible for the idea of cluster development. Index.

423. **Wild America.** 1+ March 1979+ Denver, Colo., American Wilderness Alliance. Quarterly

A journal published by a new organization whose objectives include studying the relationships between humanity and wilderness. The first issue contains part I of "The Future of Wilderness—the Need for a Philosophy," by Roderick Nash.

424. **Wilderness: America's Living Heritage.** Proceedings of the 7th Biennial Wilderness Conference, San Francisco, 1960. Edited by David Brower. San Francisco: Sierra Club, 1961. 204 p.

Much of this Conference was devoted to discussions of the meaning of wilderness. See especially papers by William O. Douglas, Sigurd Olson, and Joseph W. Krutch. Black and white photographs.

425. **Wilderness in a Changing World.** Proceedings of the 9th Biennial Wilderness Conference, San Francisco, 1965. Edited by Bruce M. Kilgore. San Francisco: Sierra Club, 1966. 251 p.

This volume commemorates the birth of the National Wilderness System and the death of Howard Zahniser. The theme as stated in the keynote address is that there is a common desire and need for wilderness. See especially the address by Albert E. Burke, "The Spirit of the Place." Black and white photographs.

426. Wogaman, J. Philip. **The Great Economic Debate: An Ethical Analysis.** Philadelphia: Westminster Press, 1977. 182 p.

Written by a theologian as a guide to Christian thinking and as an aid in choosing options in society's present debate: how should economic life be organized. Wogaman underscores moral values and the need for a new global consciousness. See especially chapters 1. "Is Economics Beyond Morality?"; 3. "Moral Foundations"; and 9. "Ideology and Beyond."

427. Woodcock, Leonard. **Labor and the Politics of Environment.** Sierra Club Bulletin 56(10) December 1971: 11–16.

Condensation of testimony before the Subcommittee on Air and Water Pollution, U. S. Senate, June 28, 1971. A union leader demonstrates how environmental quality and social justice can only be achieved by a new social and environmental ethic which must be forced on industry by government.

428. **The Works of Thy Hands: Scripture for Reflection in an Age of Environmental Crisis.** Prepared by Rodney F. Allen, Daniel M. Ulrich, and Carmelo P. Foti. Winona, Minn.: St. Mary's College Press, 1973. 89 p.

Basic questions leading to self-examination are set forth in an illustrated text. Black and white photographs illuminate appropriate quotations from the Old and New Testaments.

429. World Council of Churches. **Work Book for the Fifth Assembly of Churches, Nairobi, Kenya, 23 November–10 December 1975.** 176 p.

An aid to preparation for the conference and a guide to the program, with background information on the ecumenical movement. See especially section VI: "Human Development: The Ambiguities of Power, Technology, and the Quality of Life."

430. Worster, Donald. **Nature's Economy: The Roots of Ecology.** San Francisco: Sierra Club, 1977. 404 p.

A cultural historian investigates the course of environmental thought over the past two hundred years. Consideration of the "economy of Nature" reflects society's changing concerns: economic, religious, intellectual. This account describes dramatic shifts of viewpoint—the imperial ethic, the schools of arcadianism, mechanism, organicism, transcendentalism—and the key figures who represent the disciplines that have contributed to the "new ecology" in its most recent scientific phase. Glossary; extensive bibliography; index.

431. Wright, Cedric. **Words of the Earth.** San Francisco: Sierra Club, 1960. 93 p.

Poetic text and beautiful photographs attest to the meaning of earth's wilderness and make a strong case for educating for conservation ethics.

432. Zimmer, Heinrich R. **Philosophies of India.** Edited by
Joseph Campbell. New York: Published for Bollingen
Foundation by Pantheon Books, 1951. 687 p.

Compiled and edited posthumously. This volume brings together materials
on many phases of Indian philosophy into three broad sections: foundations; the philosophies of time; the philosophies of eternity. See especially
pp. 576–580 for a Tāntric explanation of the man-nature relationship.
Illustrations; bibliography; a general and a Sanskrit index.

433. Zuck, Robert K. **Conservation and Ecology.** Drew
Gateway 40(2) Winter 1970: 102–107.

A brief review of recent literature on the subject. It concludes with the
message from "Crisis in Eden" by Frederick Elder that the churches will
have to lead in guiding the affluent society toward restraint and in coun-
seling concern for all earth's inhabitants.

434. Zwick, David and Benstock, Marcy. **Water Wasteland:
Ralph Nader's Study Group Report on Water Pollution.** New
York: Grossman, 1971. 494 p.

Problems in political and economic ethics are an important secondary
feature of this Task Force study. See especially chapter 20, "Conclusions
and Recommendations," which discusses some major stumbling blocks
to eliminating environmental contamination: the political power of special
interest groups and the vulnerability of government regulators to "political
sabotage." This report offers positive suggestions to reduce some economic and psychological impasses. Introduction by Ralph Nader. Appendixes; notes; index.

435. **Zygon: A Journal of Religion and Science.** 9(4)
December 1974: 270–351.

Nearly an entire issue devoted to diverse inquiries relating to the images
of humanity, environmental concerns, relations to the land, ethical dimensions of ecology, and the relationship between scientific and religious
vision. Prime contributors are: Victor Ferkiss, Lawrence N. Gelb, William
H. Klink, Carle E. Braaten, and Hans Schwarz. There is also a summary
of Arthur Koestler's philosophy by John A. Miles. Notes.

Appendix

Other Bibliographies, Directories, and Indexes

A selected list of reference tools which might also be consulted in an extended search for material on this topic. Numerical sequence follows that of the bibliography.

436. American Association for the Advancement of Science. Office of Science Education. **EVIST Resource Directory: A Directory of Programs and Courses in the Field of Ethics and Values in Science and Technology.** Washington, D. C.: 1978. 208 p.

A guide to academic programs, courses, and personnel prepared under a grant from the National Science Foundation. The directory has three main sections and an appendix; each is further subdivided into broad subjects. Within each subject in the first section, entries are arranged alphabetically by name of the course. In the first two sections entries are annotated and full information is given on institution, address, personnel, name of course(s); in the third, the course title and name of institution only are given. There is no index.

437. Barnouw, Dorothy B. and Dickinson, Irene P. **Energy Bibliography Annotated.** Introduction by George Wald. Washington, D.C.: National Intervenors, 1978. 60 p.

A selected bibliography for the non-specialist, including background material on creation of earth, formation of fossil fuels, and philosophical and economic aspects. The compilation is divided into: "Nuclear Background" and "Solar Energy"; entries are arranged alphabetically by author. Number of pages is not usually given; prices are. Two lists complete the volume—"Journals Where Energy Articles may Usually be Found" and "Organizations Which can Supply Additional Information." Available from the publisher at 1413 K St., N.W., Washington, D.C. 20005.

438. **Dissertation Abstracts International.** v. 1+ 1938+ Ann Arbor, Mich.: University Microfilms. Frequency varies.

Abstracts of doctoral dissertations from U.S., Canadian, and European universities. Currently issued monthly and cumulated. Each issue has two parts—humanities and social sciences, and sciences and engineering—and is arranged by subject, and under the subject, alphabetically by author.

There are author and keyword title indexes which are cumulated annually. Dissertations are available by purchase either on microfilm or xerographic copies.

439. **Environment.** Library Journal 103(9) May 1, 1978+
Annual.
The May issue of this journal lists books on environmental topics to be published May–September of each year. Entries are arranged alphabetically by author and include title, publisher, with address if obscure, month to be published, price, and ISBN number.

440. **The Human Environment.** v. I. Washington, D.C.:
Woodrow Wilson International Center for Scholars, 1972.
171 p.
A selective, annotated bibliography of reports and documents on international environmental problems. In addition to reports and documents, this bibliography also includes books, journal articles, and theses. It contains references to the many aspects of environmental ethics. The arrangement is by format and issuing agency, except the Miscellaneous section, which is alphabetical by author. Full bibliographic information is included. Key word subject index.

441. Minneapolis Public Library. Environmental
Conservation Library. **Book Catalog,** 1974. 201 p.
A computer-produced catalog, as of 1973, representing publications in all fields which relate to the natural environment and the human impact upon it. The volume has several sections. The first lists environmental reference tools, with detailed descriptions. The next three comprise author, subject, and title catalogs to the Library collection; information includes author, title, and date in each section; the author catalog gives publisher also. Two appendixes complete the volume; the more pertinent lists periodicals (including newsletters) and is arranged alphabetically by title. It includes initial date, frequency, price, name, and address of publisher.

442. Owings, Loren C. **Environmental Values, 1860–1972: A**
Guide to Information Sources. Detroit: Gale, 1972. 324 p.
A selected, annotated bibliography on attitudes in the United States. The introduction points out that from the development of interest in conservation has come an environmental ethic. Arrangement is by general subject or by type of writing. Author, title, and subject index.

443. **Reading List on Man and His Environment.** Journal of
Environmental Education 4(1) Fall 1972: 7–9.
An annotated list compiled by several members of the Conservation Foundation and other organizations. Arranged by broad subjects, it gives full bibliographic information, noting which titles are available in paperback.

444. **Religion Index.** v. 1+ July–December 1977+. American Theological Library Association. Semi-annual.

Formerly "Index to Religious Periodical Literature," 1949–1976. Cumulation issued biennially. In three sections. First, a subject index to religious periodical literature. Second, an author index with abstracts. Not all entries listed in the first section are abstracted. Entries include volume, paging, and date. Special emphasis is given to articles in the English language but those in other languages, mainly Western European, are also indexed. Third section is book review index arranged by author and title. Volume 12 lists the journals currently being indexed.

445. Siehl, George H. **Environment Update.** Library Journal 95(8) April 15, 1970+

Annual review of environmental literature and developments by a staff member of the Congressional Research Service. It consists of brief notes on current events, followed by critical comments on current publications. Information usually includes author, title, and publisher. Title and issue number vary.

446. Stange, Douglas C. **A Bibliography on Religion and Ecology for Lutherans.** The Lutheran Quarterly 23(4) November 1971: 329–334.

An unannotated list arranged alphabetically by author.

Sources Consulted

American Association for the Advancement of Science, Washington, D.C.

Catholic University of America, Washington, D.C.

The Conservation Foundation, Washington, D.C.

District of Columbia Public Library System, Washington, D.C.

General Theological Seminary, New York, N.Y.

Library of Congress, Washington, D.C.

National Council of the Churches of Christ, New York, N.Y.

National Intervenors, Washington, D.C.

National Wildlife Federation, Washington, D.C.

Rachel Carson Council, Inc., Washington, D.C.

Union Theological Seminary, New York, N.Y.

U. S. Department of the Interior Library, Washington, D.C.

Woodrow Wilson International Center for Scholars, Washington, D.C.

Subject Index

By entry number

Aesthetics   69, 76, 87, 107, 122, 142, 145, 157, 165, 189, 219, 240, 250, 281, 344, 346, 398, 410, 416

Agriculture   29, 62, 151, 358, 401

Air pollution   12, 401

Animal rights   35, 143, 160, 181, 231, 282, 290, 318, 353, 399

Animals   26, 76, 97, 141, 143, 158, 160, 164, 225, 348, 359, 399

Animals, Africa   59, 275, 306

Animals, India   194

Animals, Wales   411

Anthropology   125

Art   76, 188, 189, 398, 432

Atmosphere   12

Artificial environments   62, 217, 409

Biology   14, 22, 23, 24, 118, 193, 201, 216, 237, 263, 314, 326, 339, 391, 392, 410

Birds   161, 373

Buddhism   113, 117, 133, 292, 340, 350

Business   29, 60, 73, 90, 103, 116, 165, 192, 204, 236, 358, 360, 374, 404, 427

Christianity, historical   95, 99, 101, 129, 139, 151, 170, 186, 197, 214, 420

Church   1, 13, 15, 17, 20, 64, 71, 72, 81, 87, 89, 93, 96, 100, 101, 107, 114, 117, 119, 120, 121, 126, 127, 128, 133, 137, 139, 150, 163, 184, 187, 191, 197, 203, 204, 209, 214, 233, 237, 250, 257, 258, 279, 280, 284, 295, 296, 300, 305, 319, 323, 327, 334, 339, 356, 372, 378, 394, 419, 420, 428, 429, 433, 435

Citizen action   21, 34, 60, 64, 72, 109, 169, 195, 203, 372, 387

Conservation   8, 18, 19, 32, 33, 44, 46, 48, 65, 82, 91, 95, 96, 101, 108, 109, 132, 142, 145, 147, 148, 154, 156, 157, 163, 165, 169, 172, 188, 198, 199, 207, 218, 220, 222, 230, 242, 246, 260, 263, 271, 277, 285, 299, 301, 321, 328, 331, 343, 344, 357, 362, 366, 373, 403, 430, 433

Conservation, Africa   275, 306

Conservation, Australia   147, 205

Conservation, India   75, 345

Conservation, New Zealand   365

Conservation, Pakistan   272

Conservation, Southeast Asia   342

Conservation, U.S.S.R.   85, 251, 311

Culture, eastern   75, 76, 79, 129, 130, 136, 214, 225, 268, 278, 293, 300, 322, 327, 357, 366, 395, 413

Culture, western   28, 29, 33, 47, 74, 76, 79, 108, 129, 130, 132, 151, 186, 191, 208, 212, 214, 222, 224, 225, 228, 242, 255, 259, 260, 264, 268, 274, 276, 277, 278, 293, 300, 301, 315, 322, 327, 329, 330, 333, 346, 357, 366, 381, 395, 399, 413, 430

Cybernetics   24, 258, 295, 406

Decision making   9, 10, 12, 41, 195, 220, 280, 313, 350, 355, 364, 401, 415, 417

Economics   77, 80, 103, 116, 123, 169, 198, 204, 208, 210, 215, 261, 264, 271, 273, 309, 338, 340, 376, 387, 389, 391, 415, 426, 434

Education   5, 7, 8, 13, 22, 24, 37, 41, 83, 91, 134, 143, 149, 153, 165, 195, 203, 216, 262, 285, 302, 363, 379, 428, 431

Education, youth   5, 13, 14, 22, 23, 43, 55, 93, 193, 200, 216, 253, 262, 310, 384, 386

Name Index

Individual and corporate names not appearing as primary authors; by entry number